LEARN PENCIL DRAWING AND COLORING

- Education Based Art Book -

NONGDAMBA LEITANTHEM

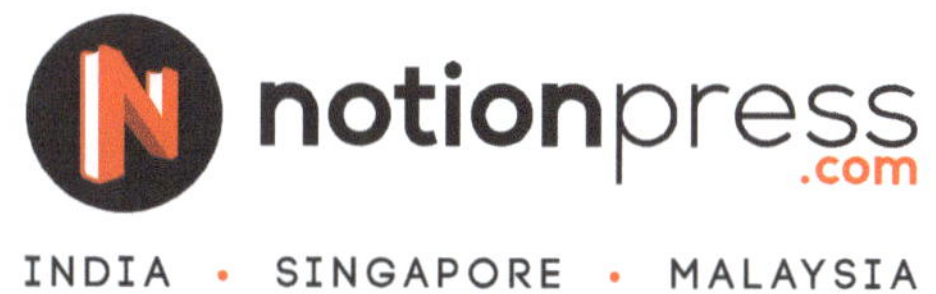

notionpress.com

INDIA · SINGAPORE · MALAYSIA

ISBN 979-8-89446-001-7

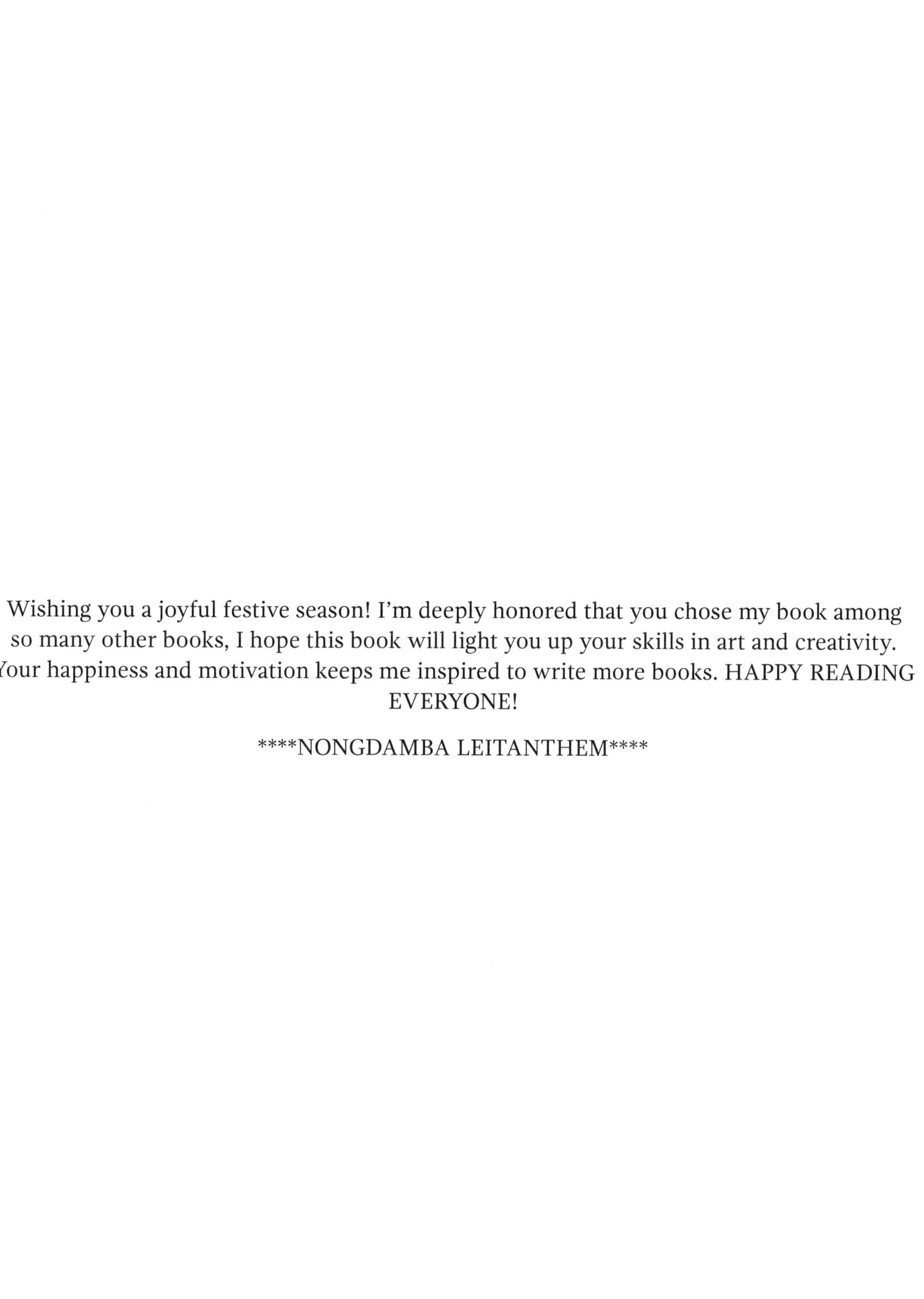

Wishing you a joyful festive season! I'm deeply honored that you chose my book among so many other books, I hope this book will light you up your skills in art and creativity. Your happiness and motivation keeps me inspired to write more books. HAPPY READING EVERYONE!

****NONGDAMBA LEITANTHEM****

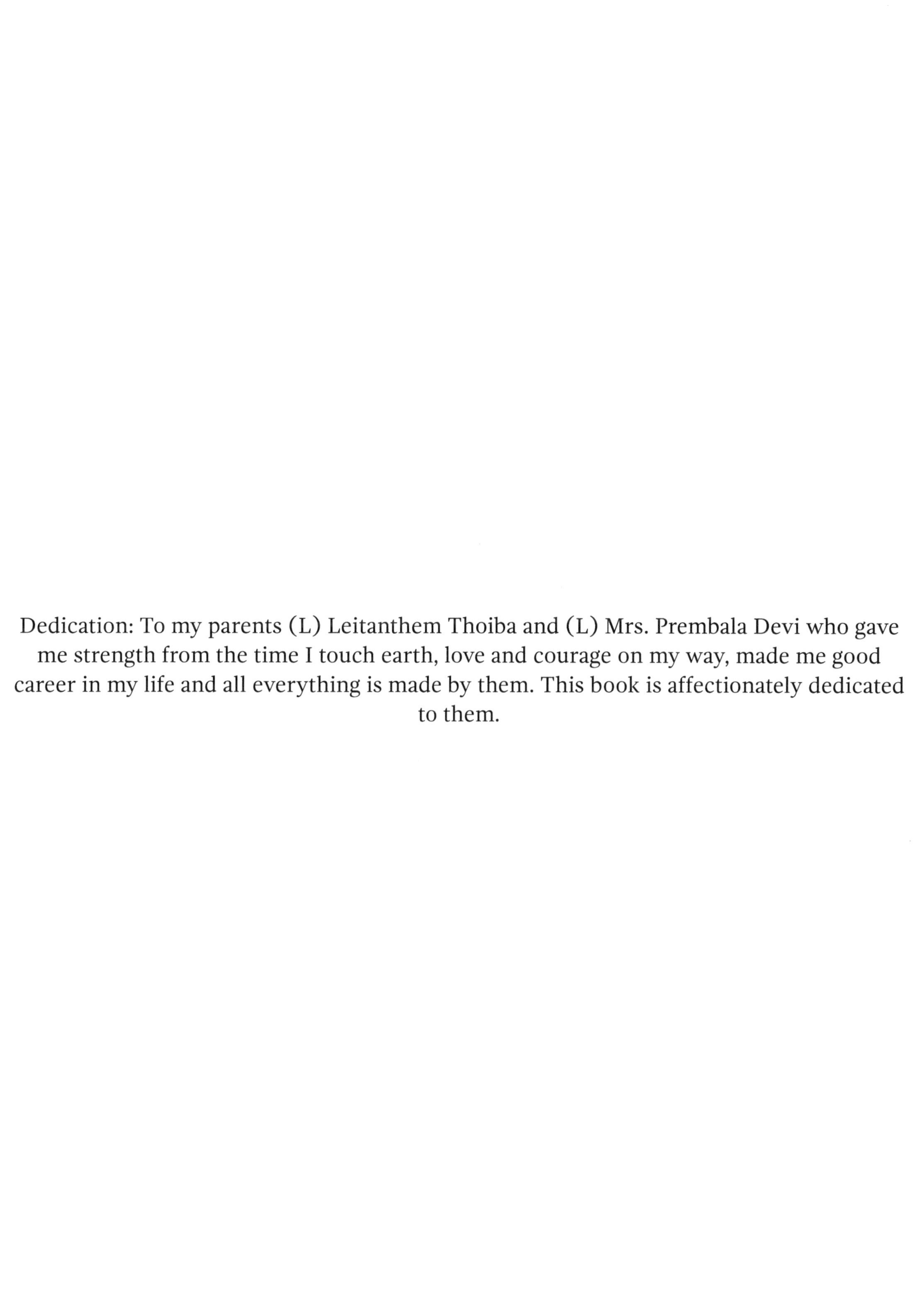

Dedication: To my parents (L) Leitanthem Thoiba and (L) Mrs. Prembala Devi who gave me strength from the time I touch earth, love and courage on my way, made me good career in my life and all everything is made by them. This book is affectionately dedicated to them.

Acknowledgement

Publishing book cannot be done by single person though having skills in hand. Lot of contribution is required from surrounding people to add value and make it possible. Big thanks to my Art teacher Yumnam Gunindro Singh for lighting me up to this stage. Thanks to Mrs. Reena Potsangbam for support to make this book. I immensely grateful to parents (L) Mr. Leitanthem Thoiba Singh and (L)Mrs. Prembala Devi for full support & encouragement. I would like to extend big thanks to my brothers, sisters, Donth Remmei and Dr. Maibam Robinson Singh who have encouraged & motivated me to publish this book.

Introduction

Drawing is one of the important field of art. Anybody can draw any picture, whatever you draw is art but forget your drawing is looking good or not. How to improve your drawing skills is that, draw any object then add few more related objects and see what you feel about your drawing. Sometimes draw closure shape first, then complete detailing. You may not feel that good at the first time but the second time will be much better than the first time drawing. Keep trying so that you can improve your skill and you will feel happy to see your drawing. Nobody can buy your skills. So keep in mind that regular practice will make you perfect. Here I would like to show you some simple steps of pencil drawing and coloring. No age restriction for learning art. Try to start with very simple steps. Here is showing you color pencil painting steps. Normal pencil shading techniques have shown in previous book 1 and 2.

There are lot of color pencils in different brand. Just pick up light color, medium color and dark color then start shading as shown on page 1.

Coloring step 1: Start with light color in one direction and it should be same tone.

Coloring step 2: Use any related medium color and start shading from down to upwards with dark to light tone and merge with light color, and shade with light tone to get merge.

Coloring step 3: Shade with dark colour over the medium color, shading should end in the middle of medium color with light tone. Some sample is showing on this page. Try to get same shading as shown below.

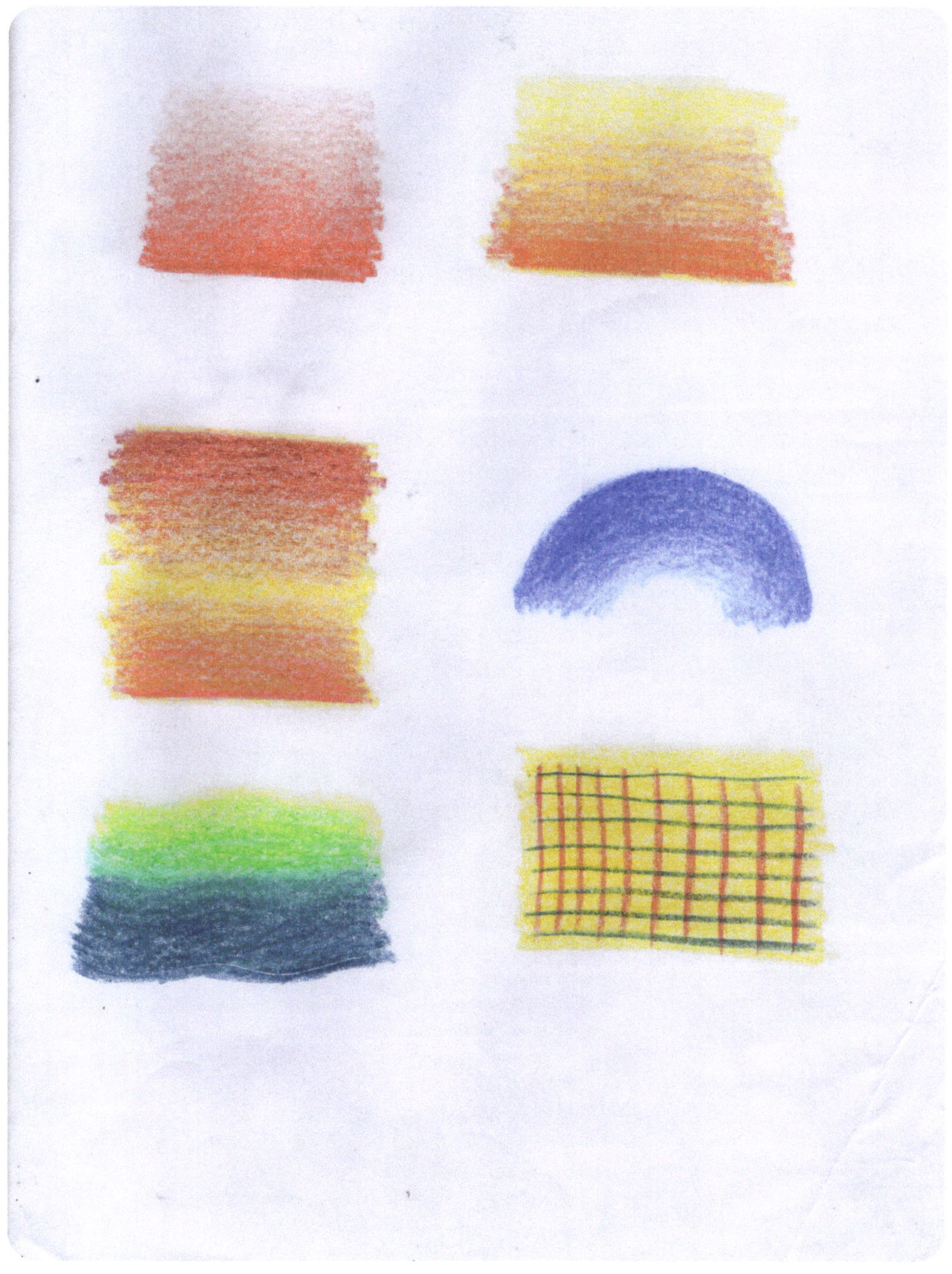

Here is showing how to draw a house from A.

Step 1: Write capital A just to start drawing of House

Step 2: Add roof at the right side of A.

Step 3: Complete drawing of House by adding wall, door and window. Anyone can draw this house after seeing this steps. Keep trying different houses.

Coloring: Any color can be used. However color in one direction, for example: If you start coloring up and down on the roof then continue doing up and down direction till complete the roof. Some of the coloring directions are here i.e. Up and down, slanting direction, Left to right etc. Two or three colors can be used for shading in every object. The way of coloring can refer from page 1.

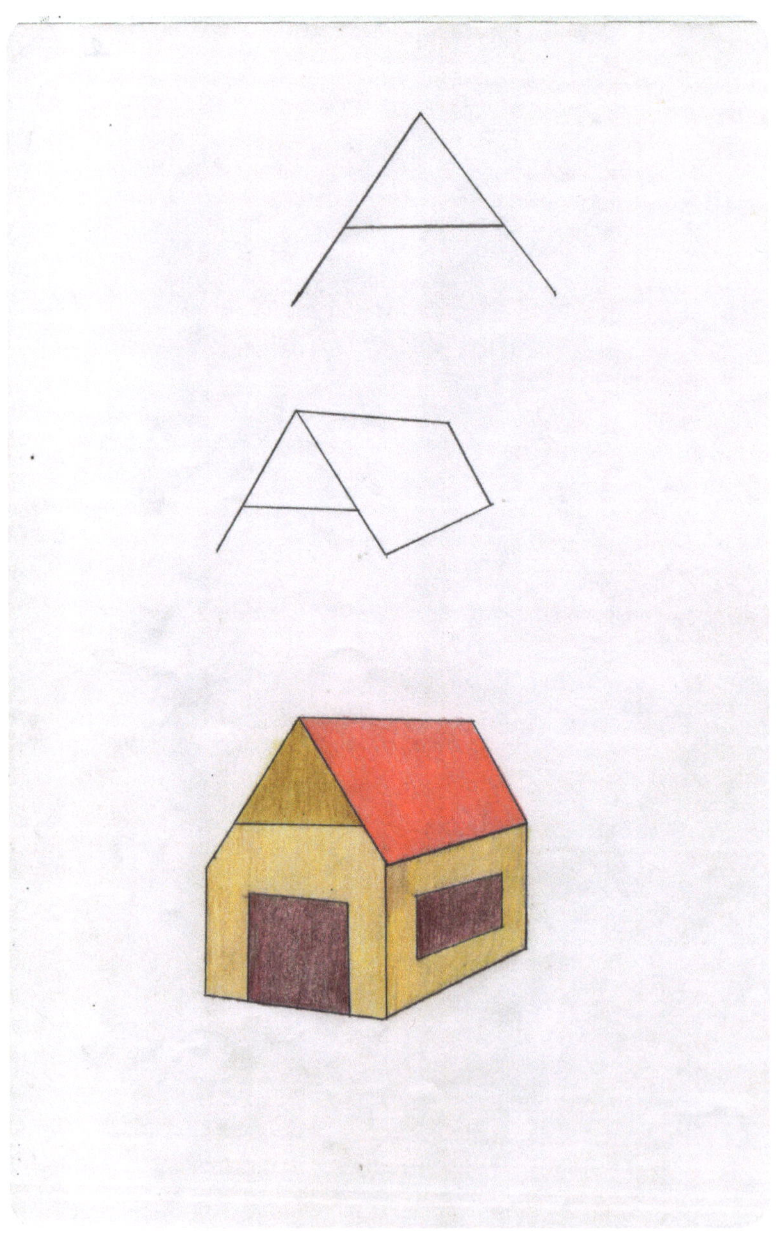

Here is showing easy way of drawing Duck from number.

Step 1: Write 2 to star drawing of Duck.

Step 2: Draw beak and part of neck.

Step 3: Complete drawing of Duck body.

Coloring: Take any color which are suitable with Duck. Always start with light color in one direction. To get light tone hold the color in the middle of the color pencil. Medium tone can start from the line of the Duck and end with light tone in the middle part of Duck. Always refer from page 1 to clarify doubts.

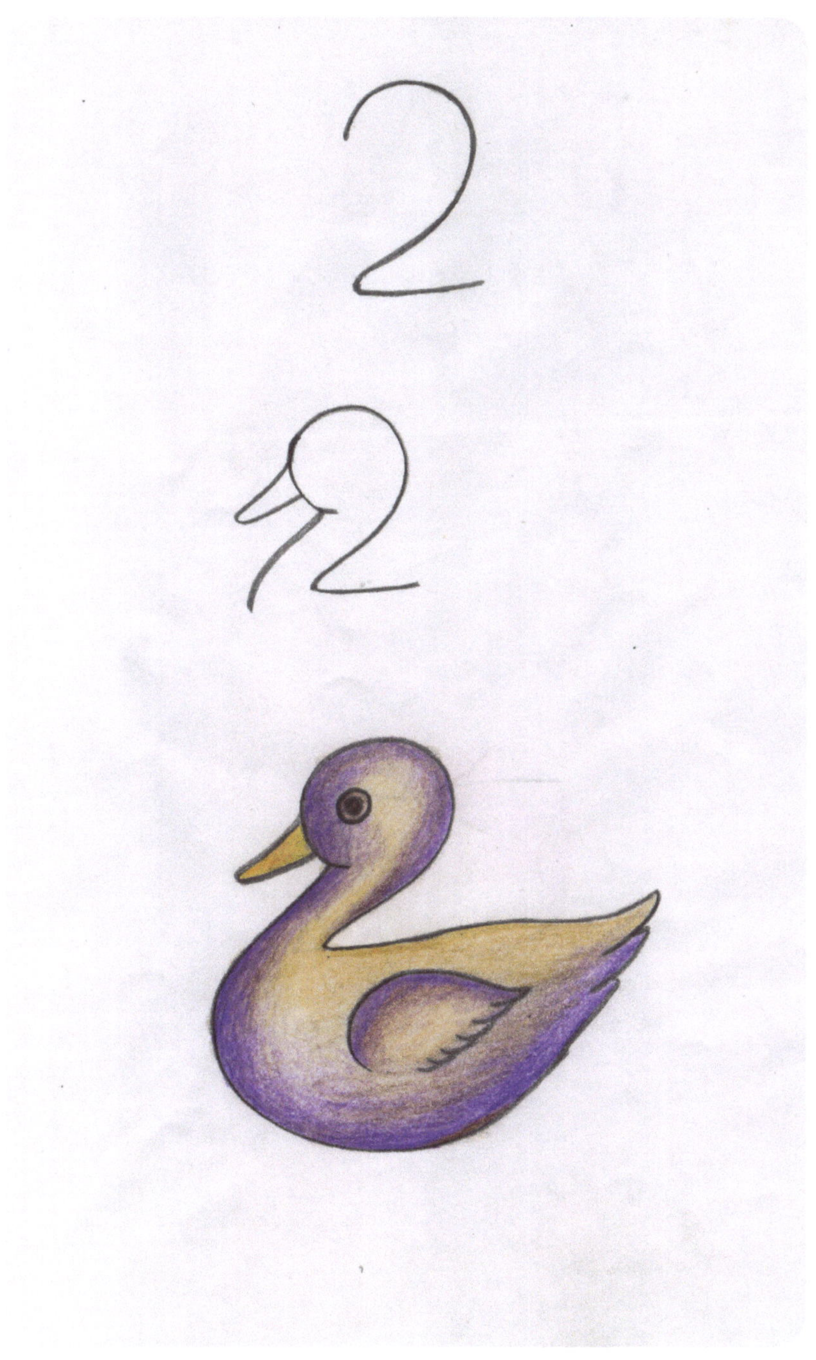

Drawing Ice cream is always easy but when we try to find out easiest way of Ice cream drawing is here.

Step 1: Draw "V" to start drawing of Ice cream.

Step 2: Draw Ice cream top over the V. Everyone can draw this Ice cream easily.

Coloring: Any color can be used as per your choice. Fill with light color tone in one direction. Continue shading with medium tone from the outer line of the Ice cream and do light tone in the middle part of the Ice cream. Refer the coloring steps from this image.

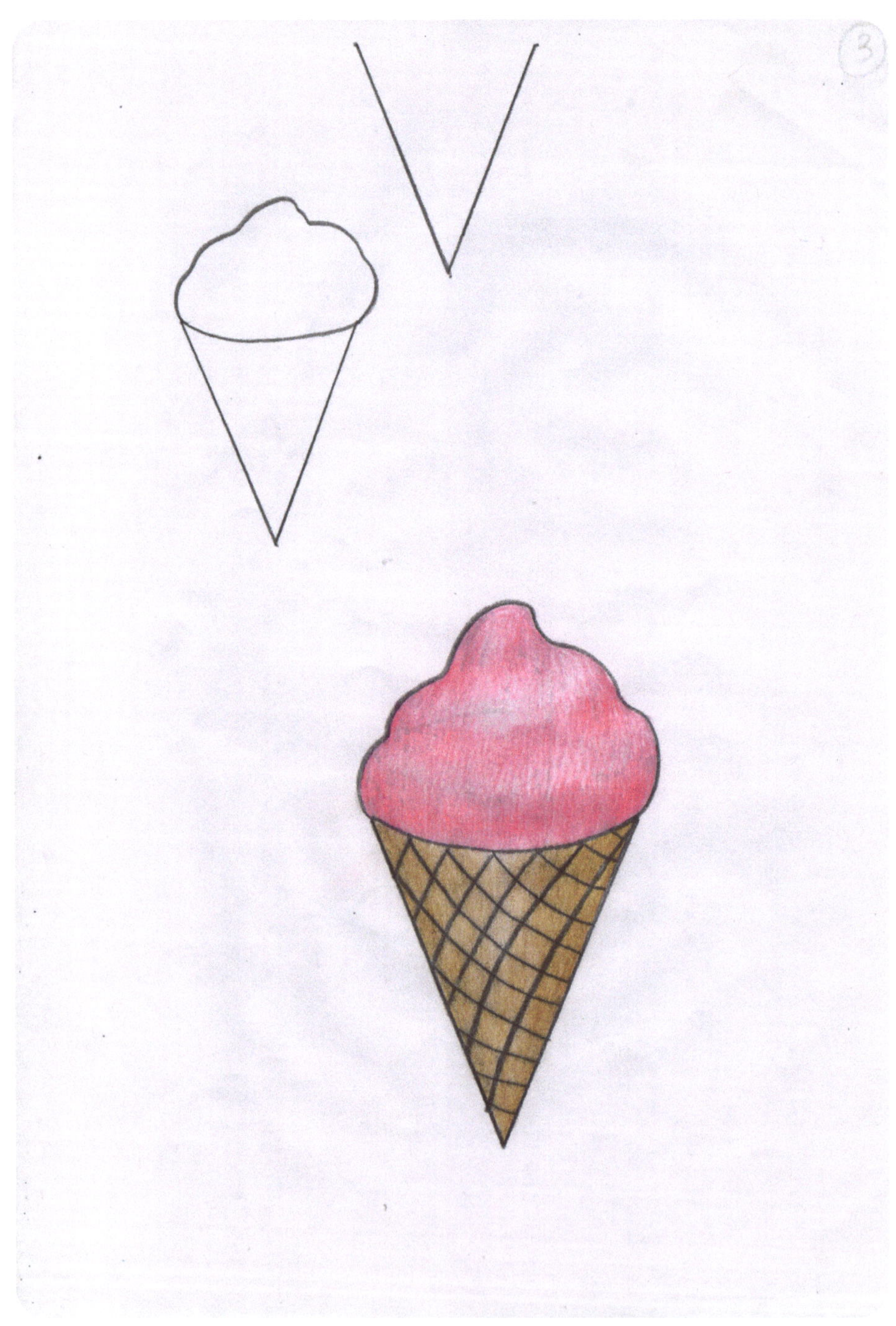

This is something interesting picture. Here is showing how to draw a Shell from a leaf. Most of the time try to get closure shape to draw any object. Closure shape is always require for beginners.

Step 1: Draw a leaf to draw Shell

Step 2: Draw upper curve line just above the leaf

Step 3: Complete drawing by adding three curve lines at the backside of the Shell.

Coloring: Fill with any light color in one direction then start shading with medium color. While using medium color should start shading from the outline then gradually reduce the darkness and merge with light color in the middle. Shading with medium color is end once merged well with light color. Final tone is with dark color, any matching dark color can use. Start shading with dark tone just above the medium color then gradually reduce the tone and merge with medium color. Picture will look good if dark color shading stop in the middle of medium color. Refer the below picture.

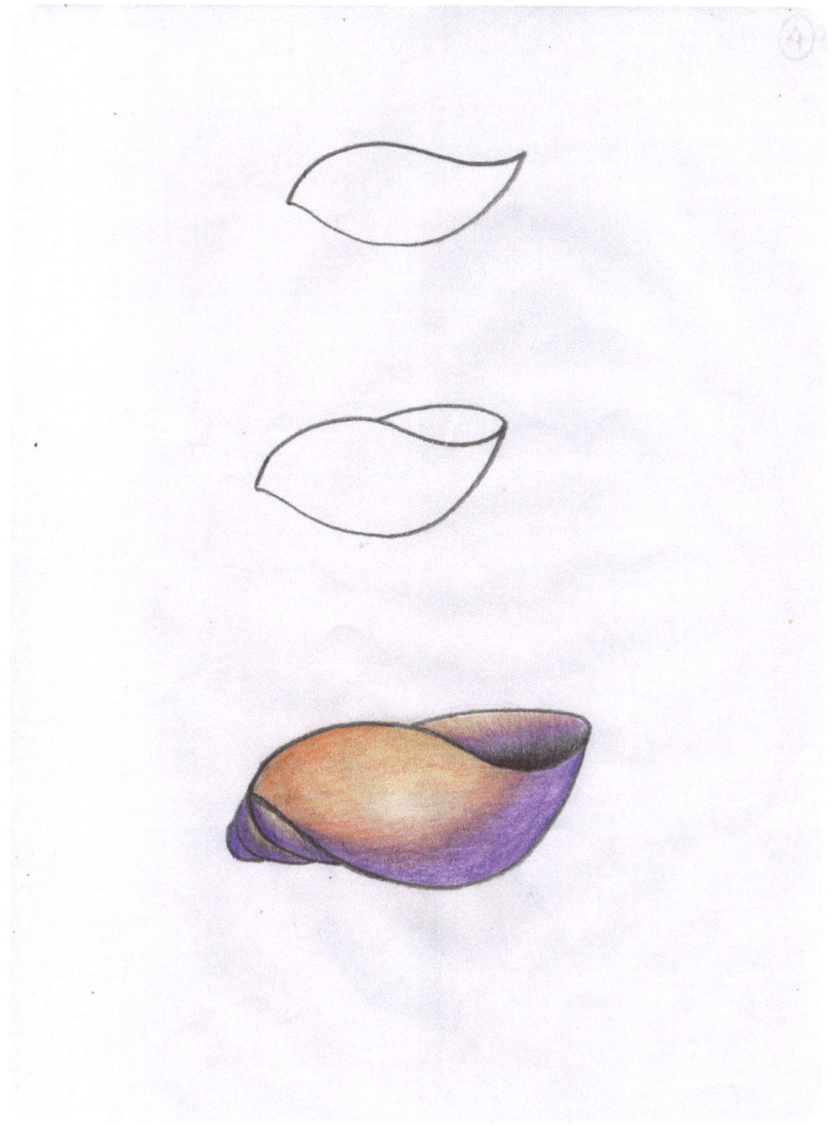

In this page is showing how to draw Kite from 4. If you look at the shape of Kite you can always get an idea to create closure shapes of an object. Let's look at the steps.

Step 1: Write 4 in big size as we are drawing Kite.

Step 2: Draw opposite L shape from the right side so that you can see a triangle shape in 4.

Step 3: Draw V and join to the left and right angle.

Coloring: Any color can be used. While coloring the pencil stroke should be in one direction. Here is done with only one color tone.

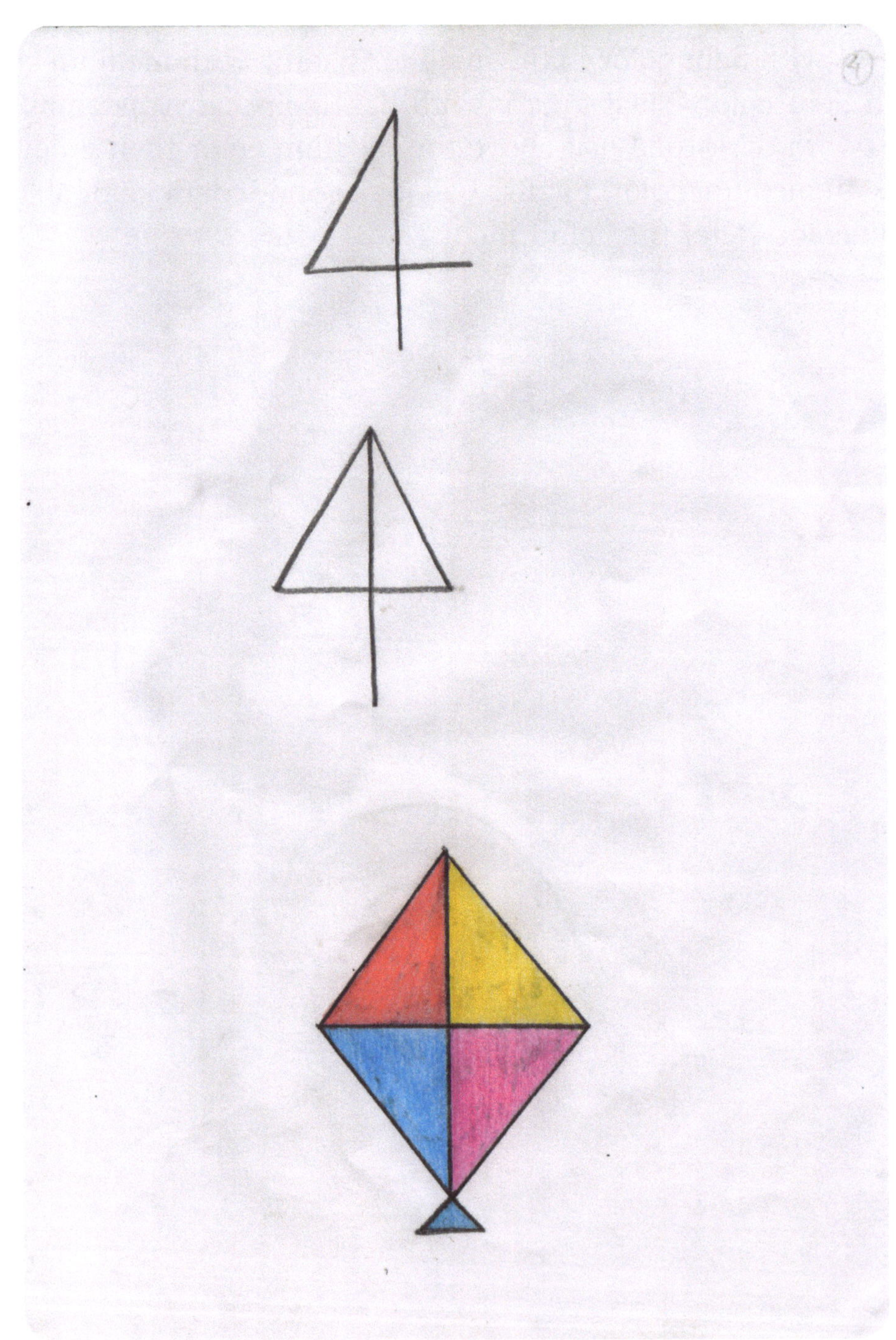

Here is showing easy way of drawing Snail. There are lot of easy steps but this is one of the easiest way of drawing Snail.

Step 1: Write 6 with proper curve line

Step 2: Extend the curve line towards right side

Step 3: Draw curve and wavy line of Snail body.

Coloring: Color can be your choice, fill with light color in one direction or according to the shape. Start shading with medium color from outline and end shading in the middle part of light color with light tone. Keep in mind that all the colors should be merged well. Then, do dark shade over the medium color and end in the middle of medium color. Refer the picture not to have doubt.

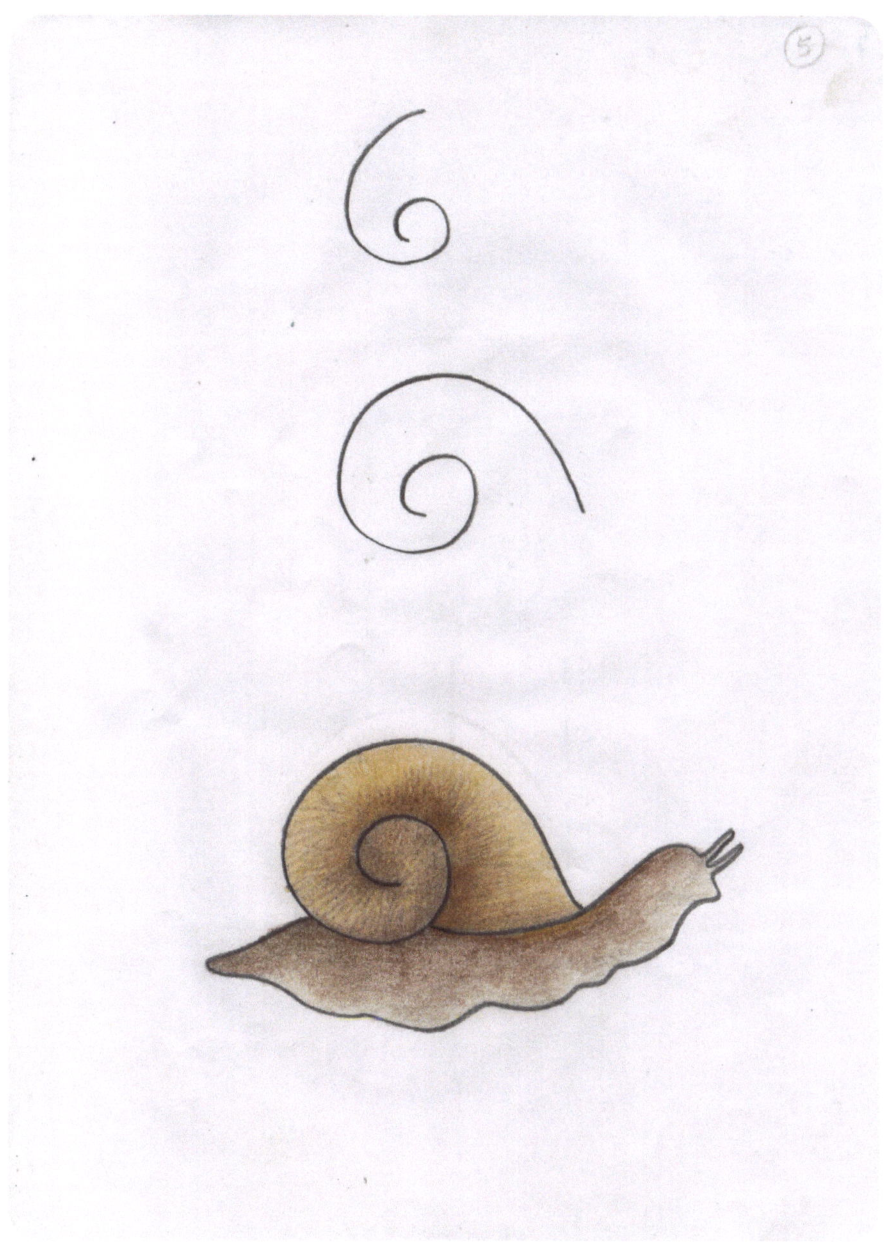

Easy way of drawing Candle is showing here.

Step 1: Write 1 in big size to draw candle.

Step 2: Draw a straight line at the left side same as shown in the picture.

Step 3: Complete drawing candle and draw flame.

Coloring: Any color can be used. Take 3 colors i.e. Dark, Medium and Light color. For color pencil start with light color first then continue with medium color and complete with dark color. Fill entire area with light color in one direction. Continue shading with medium color and end in the middle part of light color. Complete coloring with dark color. Always merge all the colors to look good.

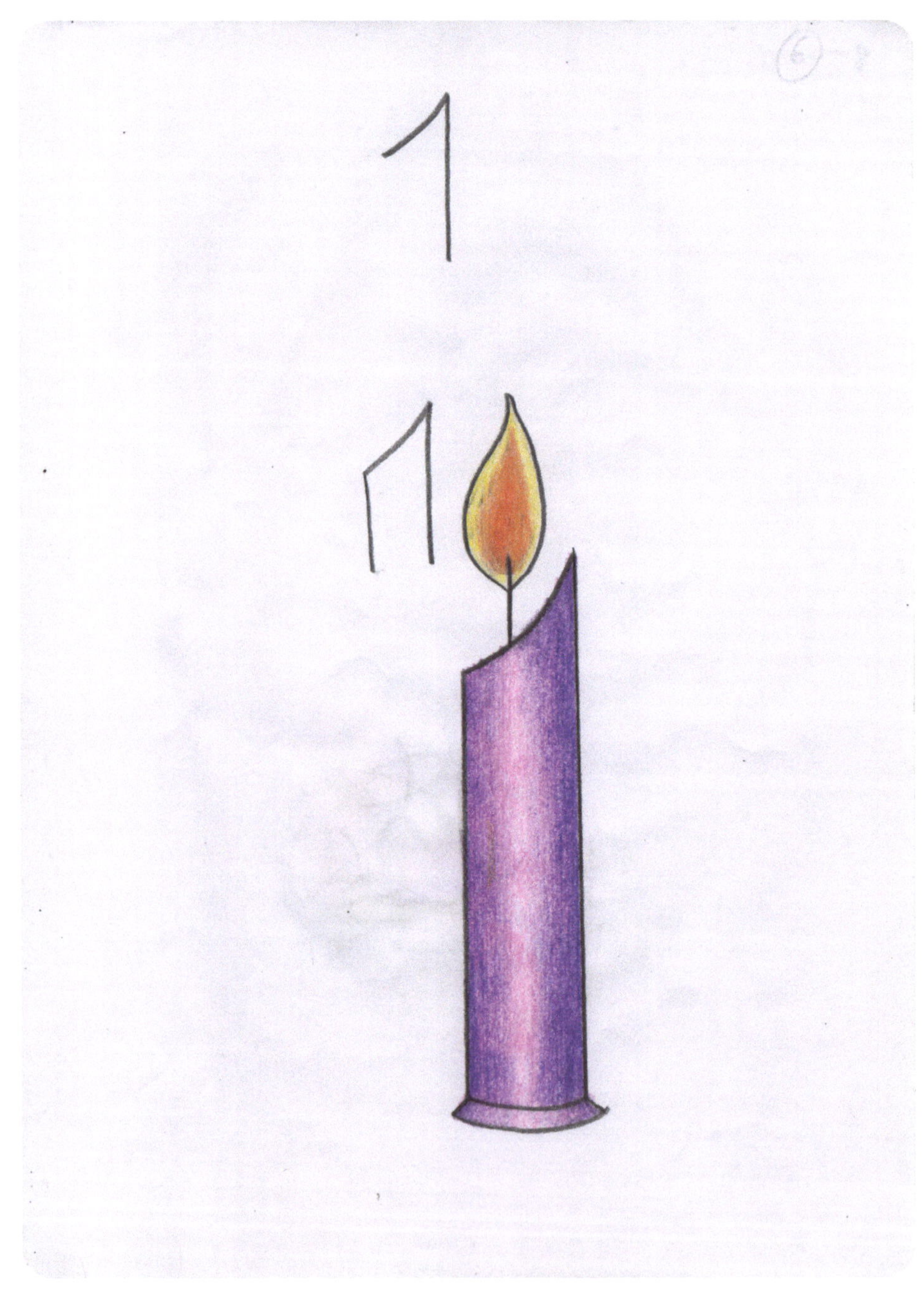

Here is showing how to draw cute Bird from C.

Step 1: Write C in big size to start drawing cute Bird.

Step 2: Draw a slanting line at the right side of C. Have a look at the picture.

Step 3: Draw the rest of parts and complete drawing.

Coloring: Any color can be used. Fill all area with light color in one direction. Start shading with medium color from the outline and continue shading with light tone till middle part of light color. Complete shading with dark color and merge all the colors.

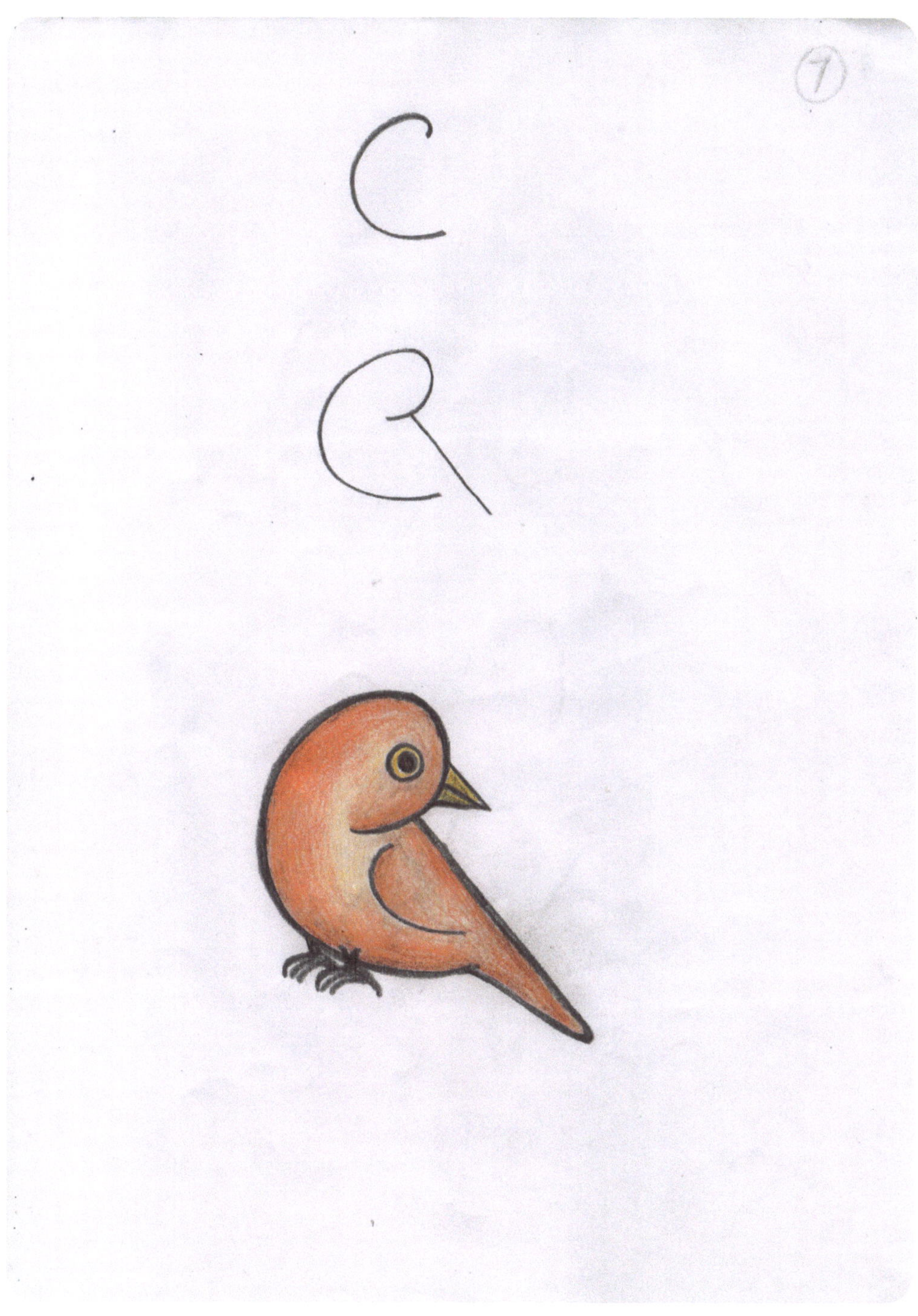

This is interesting picture. Here is showing how to draw Fish from triangle shape.

Step 1: Draw a triangle shape

Step 2: Draw another triangle shape on the right side. It should be smaller than first triangle shape.

Step 3: Draw fins, eyes and other parts of fish.

Coloring: Take any light color and fill in all area in one direction. Shade with medium color and end in the middle part of light color. Complete shading with dark color same as shown in the picture.

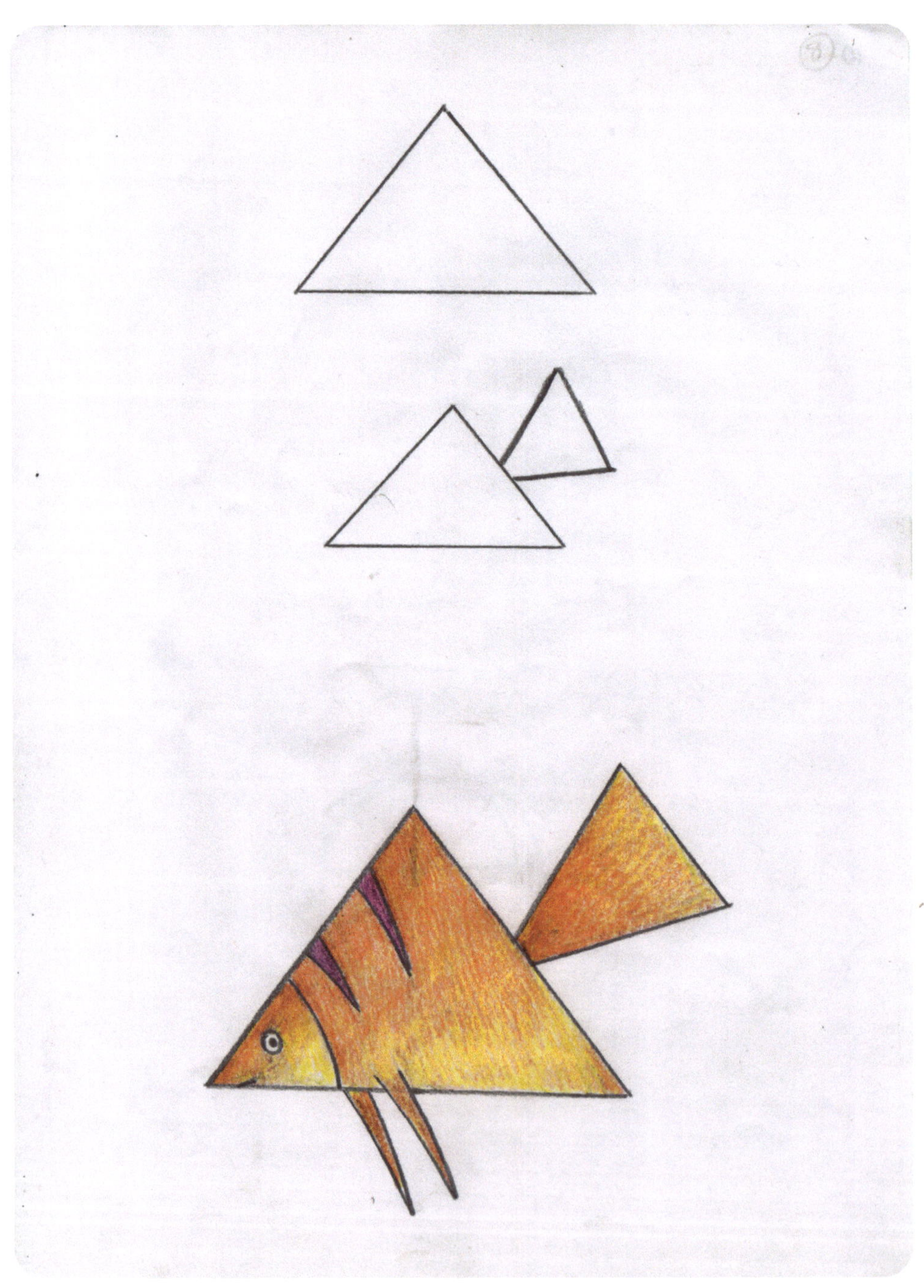

Drawing letter box from E. It is quite easy to draw letter from E.

Step 1: Write E in big size to draw letter box.

Step 2: Draw a straight line at the right side of E.

Step 3: Draw other part of letter box too.

Coloring: Any color can be used. Here is using light brown, medium brown and dark brown. Fill with light brown in all area in one direction. Start shading with medium color from the outline and end in the middle part of light color. Complete shading with dark color same as shown in the picture.

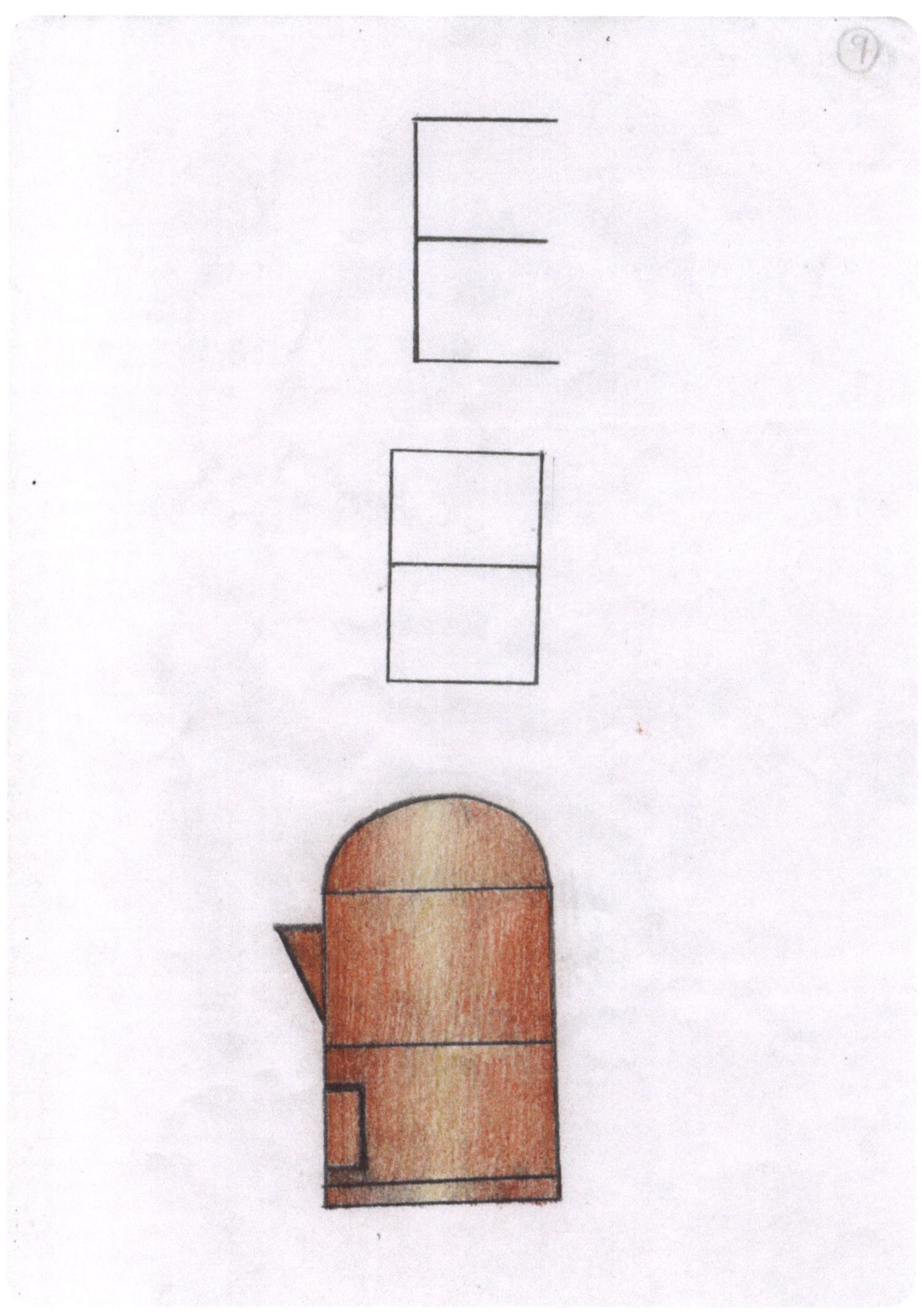

How to draw a Ball from O. Any Ball can draw from O.

Step 1: Write O in big size.

Step 2: Draw any line/design in the O.

Step 3: Complete detailing in the Ball.

Coloring: Here is using three color i.e. dark green, medium green and light green. Color with light green in all the areas in one direction. Shade with medium color from the outline and end in the middle of light color to complete shading with dark color same as shown in the picture.

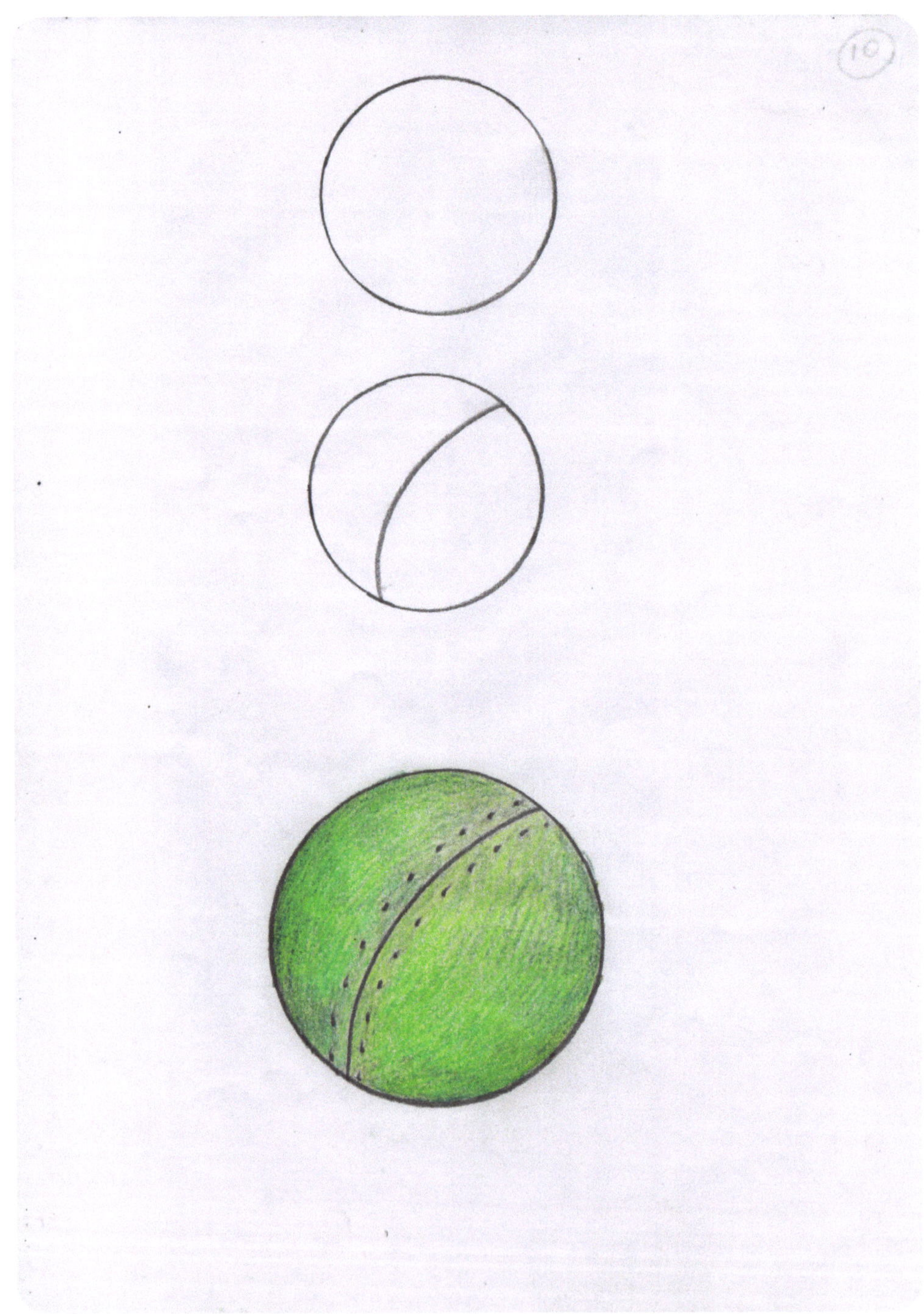

How to draw Butterfly from B is showing here.

Step 1: Write capital letter B in big size to draw Butterfly.

Step 2: Draw a small circle as Butterfly head.

Step 3: Draw two tentacles on the small circle and draw curve lines at the left side to show wing. Design your Butterfly.

Coloring: Any color can be used for Butterfly. Here is using light yellow, dark yellow and red color for the wings and blue color for body. Have a look in the picture to know the steps of coloring.

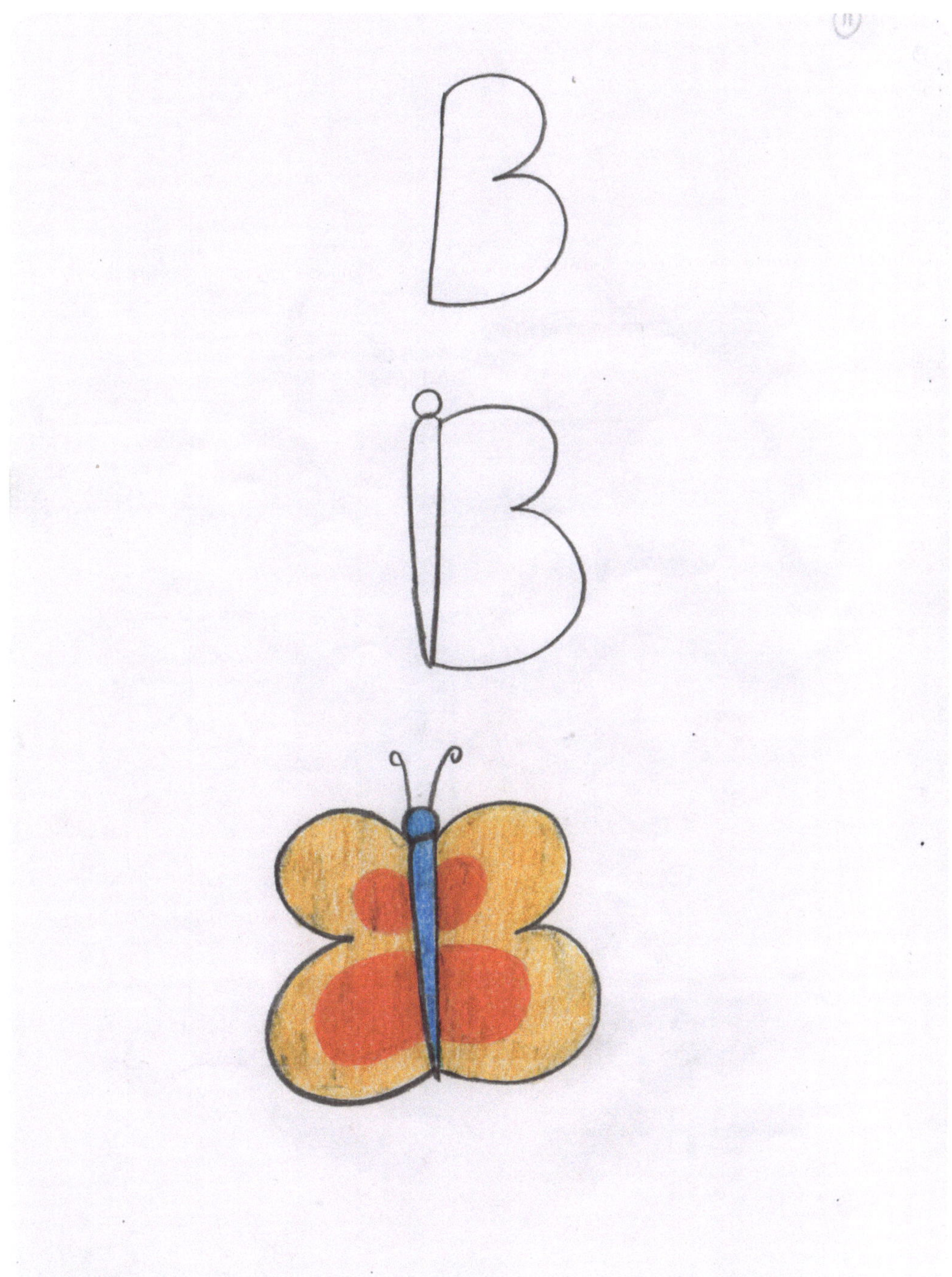

Here is showing how to draw Umbrella from J

Step 1: Write capital J in big size to draw Umbrella.

Step 2: Remove the upper part of capital J.

Step 3: Draw upside down curve line above of the capital J then draw small curve lines to complete drawing.

Coloring: Different colors can be used in all the part of Umbrella. Have a look in the picture and color the same.

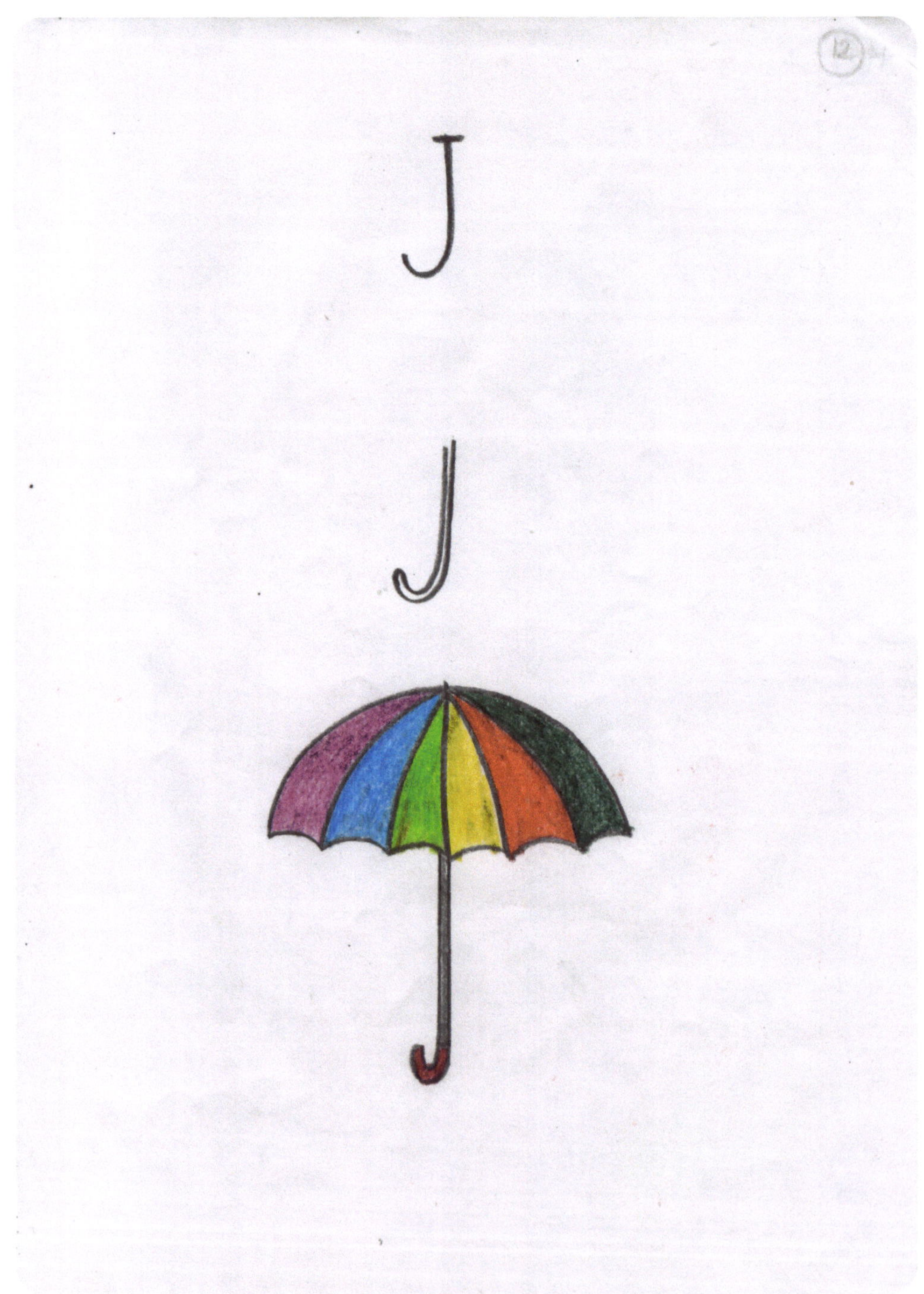

There are many ways to draw Hat but this step is quite easy to draw. Given step 1 is called closure shape. If we create closure shapes for any objects will be easier to draw. Here is showing how to draw Hat from an oval shape.

Step 1: Draw an oval shape to draw Hat. Oval shape should be according to the direction of Hat.

Step 2: Draw upper part of Hat on the oval shape.

Step 3: Draw another oval shape inside the previous oval shape.

Coloring: Using colors can be your choice. Here is using yellow, light red and dark red colors. Fill with yellow color in all areas in one direction. Shade with medium color from one side till middle part of light color. Shade with dark color over the medium color but should end at the middle of medium color. Keep in mind that all the colors should merge. Always refer given picture and try to create your own pictures.

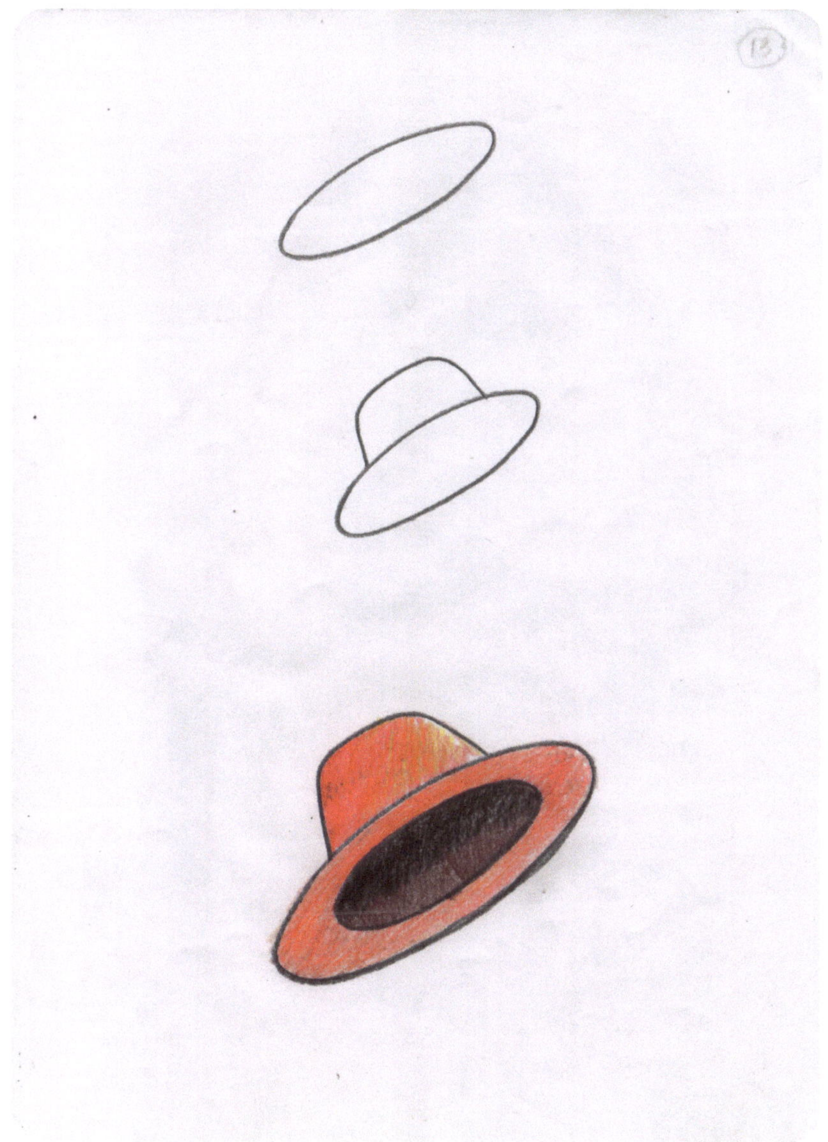

Some people cannot draw Dolphin easily. If start from closure shape will be easier for any drawing. Have a look the steps of drawing Dolphin.

Step 1: Draw closure shape of Dolphin same as showing in the book

Step 2: Add Dolphin fin and draw curve lines both the sides of fin.

Step 3: Draw tails and bottom part of Dolphin.

Coloring: Color can be similar to real Dolphin color or can make fun with color. Here is using silver color, purple color and black color. Using purple color is just to make fun not for real. Fill with silver color in all areas in one direction. Use medium color and shade from the outline, either from down to up or top to down and merge with silver color. Shade with dark color over the medium color and end in the middle of medium color. All the colors should merge well to look real. Try drawing different pose of Dolphins.

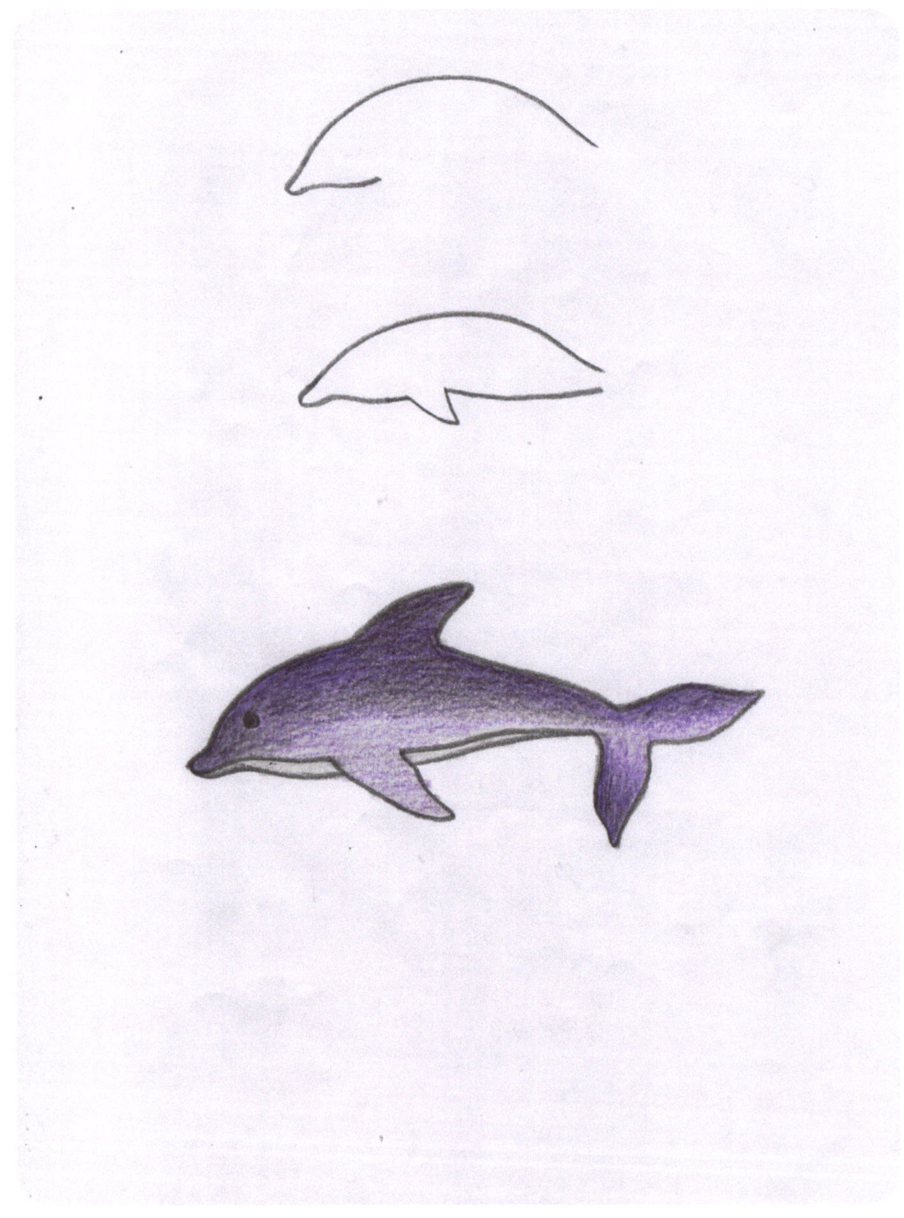

Crab is interesting picture and it's not easy to draw for some people. Here is showing how to draw crab in easy way. Always create closure shape for any objects to draw easier.

Step 1: Draw closure shape same as in the book.

Step 2: Continue drawing Crab legs same as given picture.

Step 3: Complete drawing other legs and eyes too.

Coloring: There are different colors of Crab so color is your choice. Here is using light red, medium red and dark red colors. Follow the steps of coloring. Fill with light tone in all the areas in one direction then shade with medium color from one side or from all the sides and end shading at the half of light color. Continue shading with dark color over the medium color and end shading at the half of medium color. All the colors should merge well.

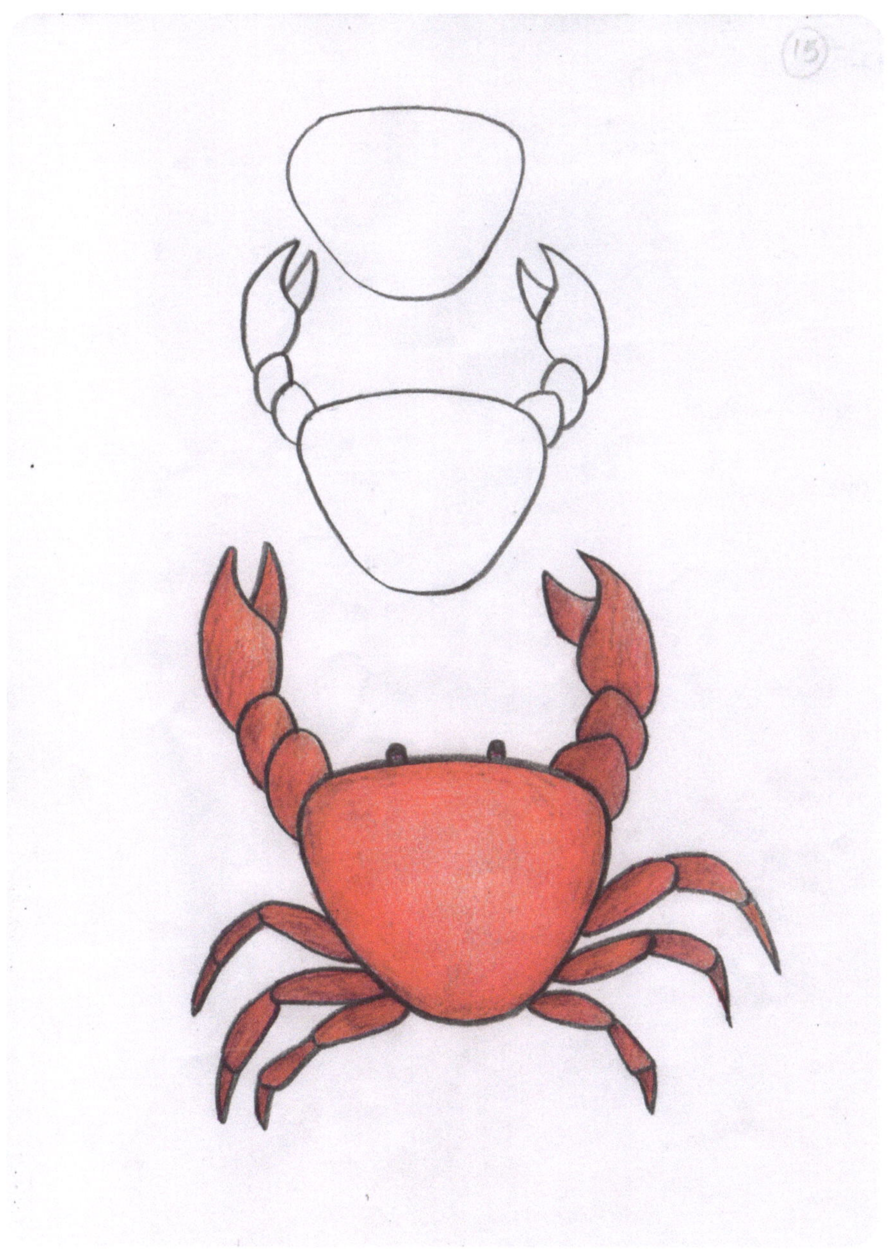

Rabbit is always cute but it's difficult to draw. Let see the steps of drawing below.

Step 1: Draw closure shape which look like head same as showing here. Also draw a circle/ oval shape for body.

Step 2: Continue drawing the upper part of Rabbit and mouth too.

Step 3: Draw legs and tail and complete the picture.

Coloring: Color is your choice. Here is using brownish tone to look fun, colors are light brown, medium brown and dark brown. Fill with light color in one direction, there should not be paper white. Shade with medium color from all the sides till half of light color. It should merge well. Shade with dark color over the medium color till half of medium color. Try different pose of Rabbit.

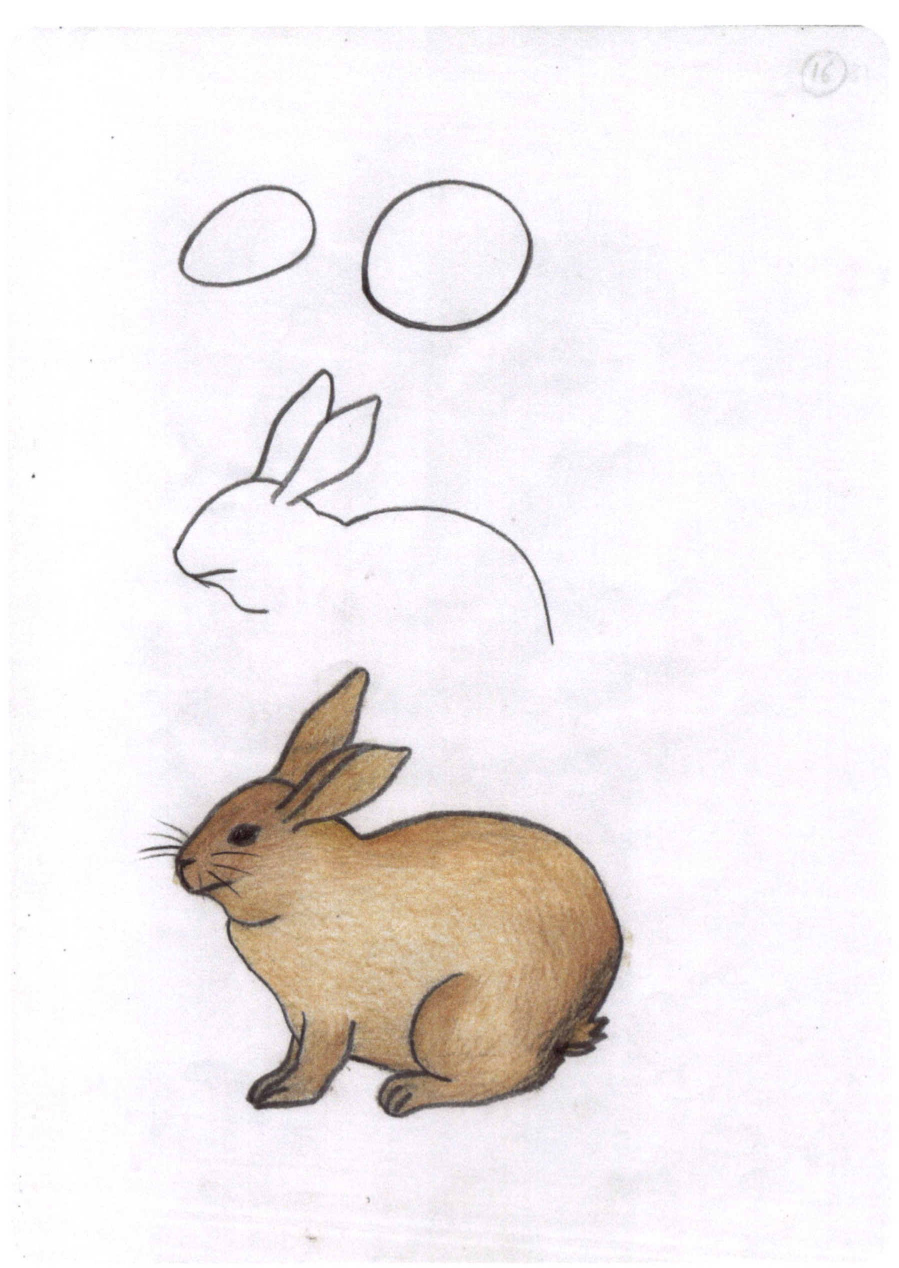

Drawing Deer is not easy, so need practice to draw Deer. Here is showing easy way of drawing Deer. Let see the steps of drawing.

Step 1: Draw closure shape same as shown in the book and draw one more rectangular shape for the body.

Step 3: Draw ears, face, horn, neck and part of body shown in the book.

Step 3: Draw legs, tail and outline of body.

Coloring: The color of Deer is brown color and white mixing. Any color can be used just to make fun with colors. Here is using light brown, medium brown and dark brown. Fill light brown in all the areas in one direction. Make sure there should not be paper white. Shade with medium color from all the sides or from any side and end the shading at the half of light color. Shade with dark color till half of medium color. All the colors should merge well.

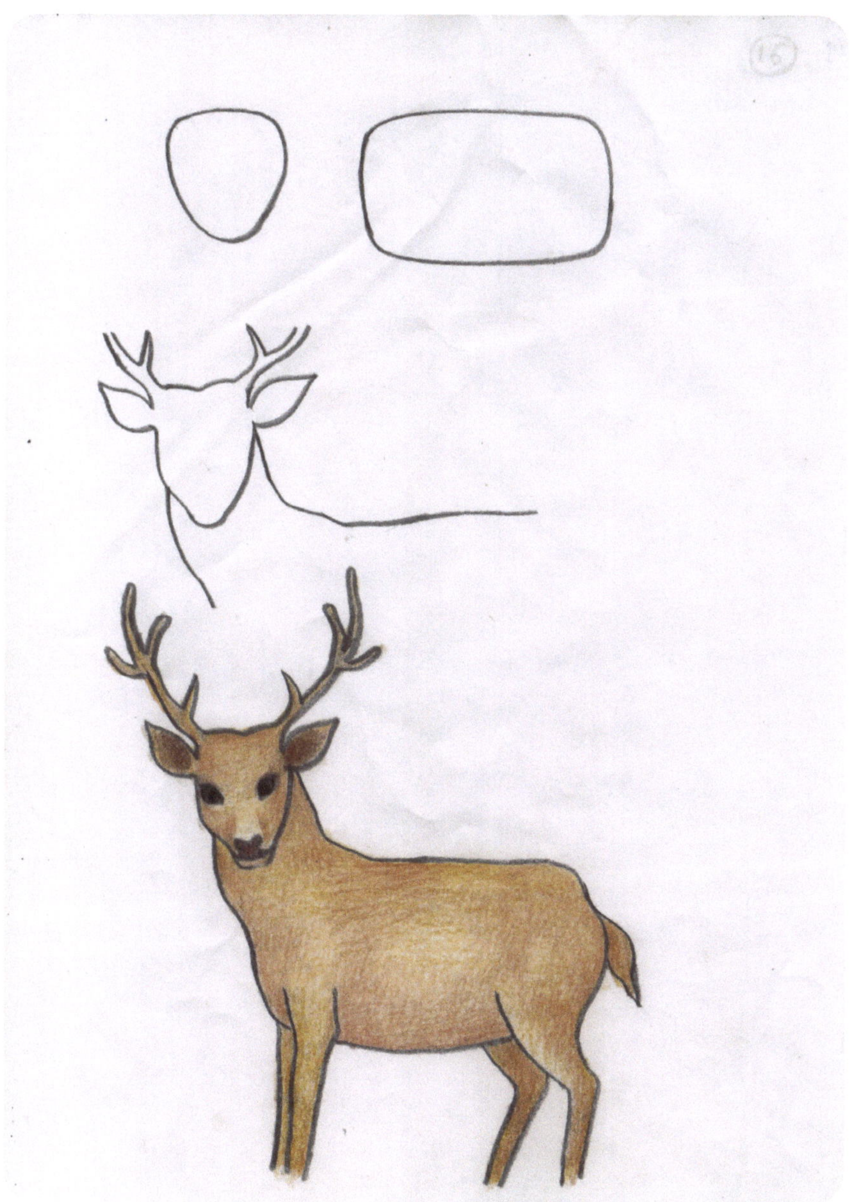

Drawing Bird is easy but sometimes difficult to draw because of different pose. Here is showing easy steps of drawing Bird. Let see the steps below.

Step 1: Draw a circle and a leaf shape for body.

Step 2: Draw proper head and also draw beak and part of body.

Step 3: Draw legs, wing, eye and tail to complete drawing Bird.

Coloring: There are many colors for Bird. So any color can pick up based on your Bird. Here is showing light violet color and black. There is white area in the body, this is paper white without coloring. Sometime we can use paper white without coloring if require. Fill with light violet color till below of wing and end with light tone to merge with paper white. Shade with black color from upper part till half of light violet color. In this picture should start shading with black from upper outline because there is white area at the bottom part of Bird. Outline is required for all the feathers in the wing and tail. We can use any color for Bird's leg.

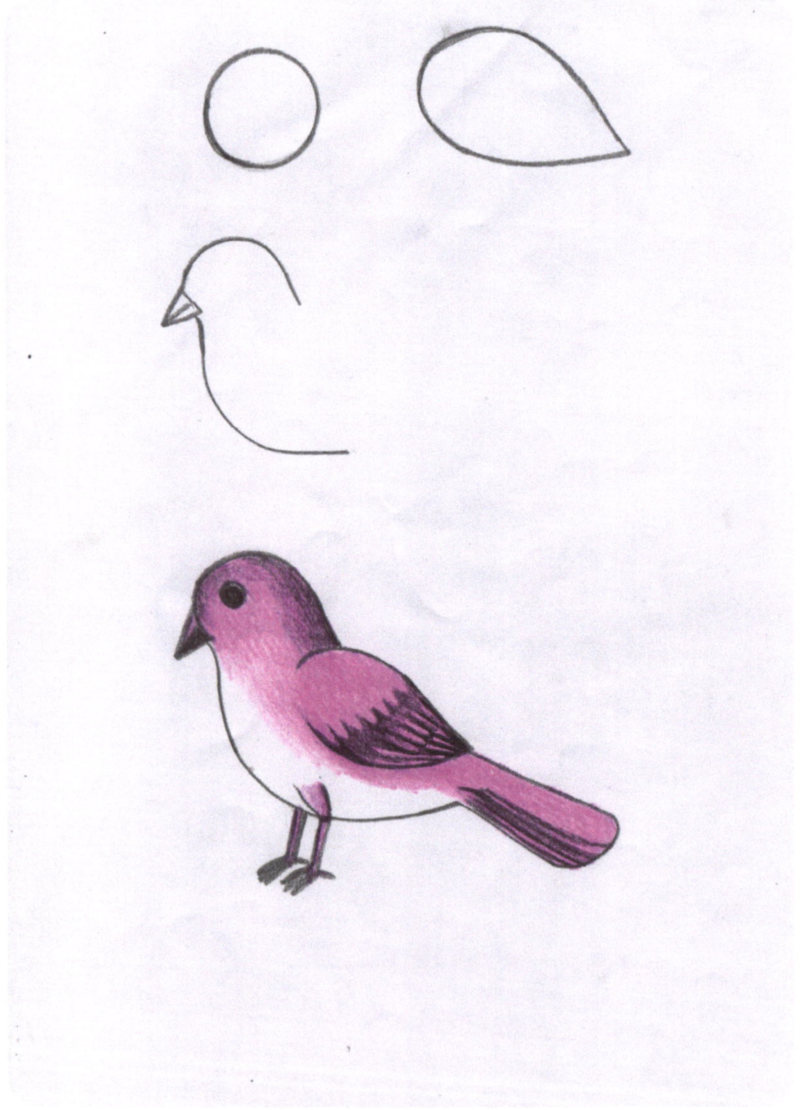

Penguin is cute animal, it's easy to draw for some people and some of them finding it difficult to draw. Here is showing easy steps of drawing Penguin. The steps are below.

Step 1: Draw an oval shape for head and draw another big oval shape for the body. Closure shapes should be based on the position of Penguin.

Step 2: Modify the Penguin shape into real from the closure shape and draw beak of Penguin.

Step 3: complete drawing with legs, tail, wing and eye etc.

Coloring: Here is using gray color for stomach of Penguin, dark brown and black color for upper part of the body, orange color for beak, yellow color for patch in the neck. Fill with gray color in one direction in the stomach. Fill dark brown in one direction in the upper part of the body and fill any colors in the rest of body. Shade with gray color from the outline till 3/4th of the gray area because Penguin is tent to white color. Shade with black color on the dark brown area, shading should be almost cover the brown color to look dark as Penguin color is black. Check the given picture not to have doubt.

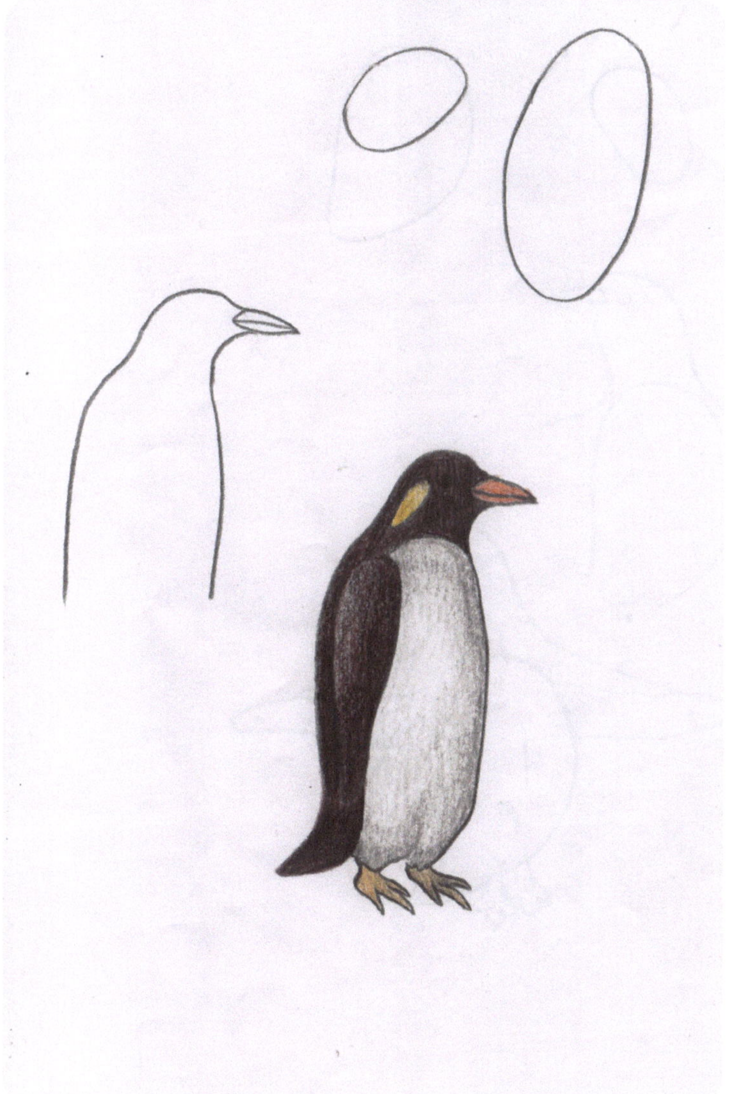

Drawing Hen is not easy but if look at Hen carefully you may find it easy to draw. Here is showing easy steps of drawing Hen. Let see the steps below.

Step 1: Draw a closure shape for head and draw another circle for body.

Step 2: Modify into real picture from the closure shape of head and body. Draw beak, feather in the neck, tail and cock comb.

Step 3: Complete drawing with legs and wing.

Coloring: There are different colors of Hen so any color can be used for Hen. Here is using light brown, medium brown and dark brown. Fill with light brown in all the areas in one direction. Shade with medium color till half of light color. Medium color shading can start from all the sides or from one side. Shade with dark color till the half of medium color. All the colors should merge well.

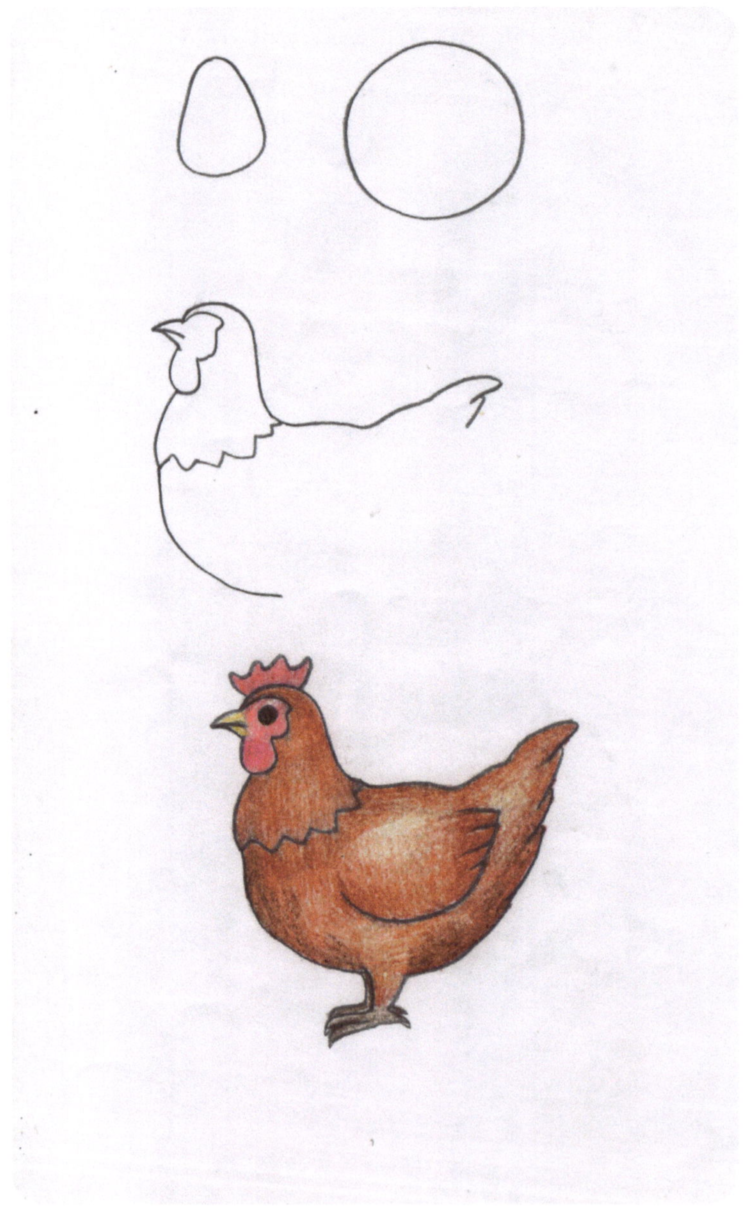

This is interesting picture but it is bit hard to draw. Let see the steps of drawing.

Step 1: Draw an oval shape for head and a circle for body.

Step 2: Modify into an Owl head and curve line from the closure shape. Draw ears as shown in the picture.

Step 3: Draw legs, wings, beak, and eyes in proper lines.

Coloring: Here is using light brown, medium brown and dark brown etc. Color with light brown in one direction, make sure no paper white while coloring. Shade with medium color with rough texture as shown in the picture. Complete with dark color over the medium area. Color the other parts also i.e. legs, eyes, beak, tree branch and claws etc.

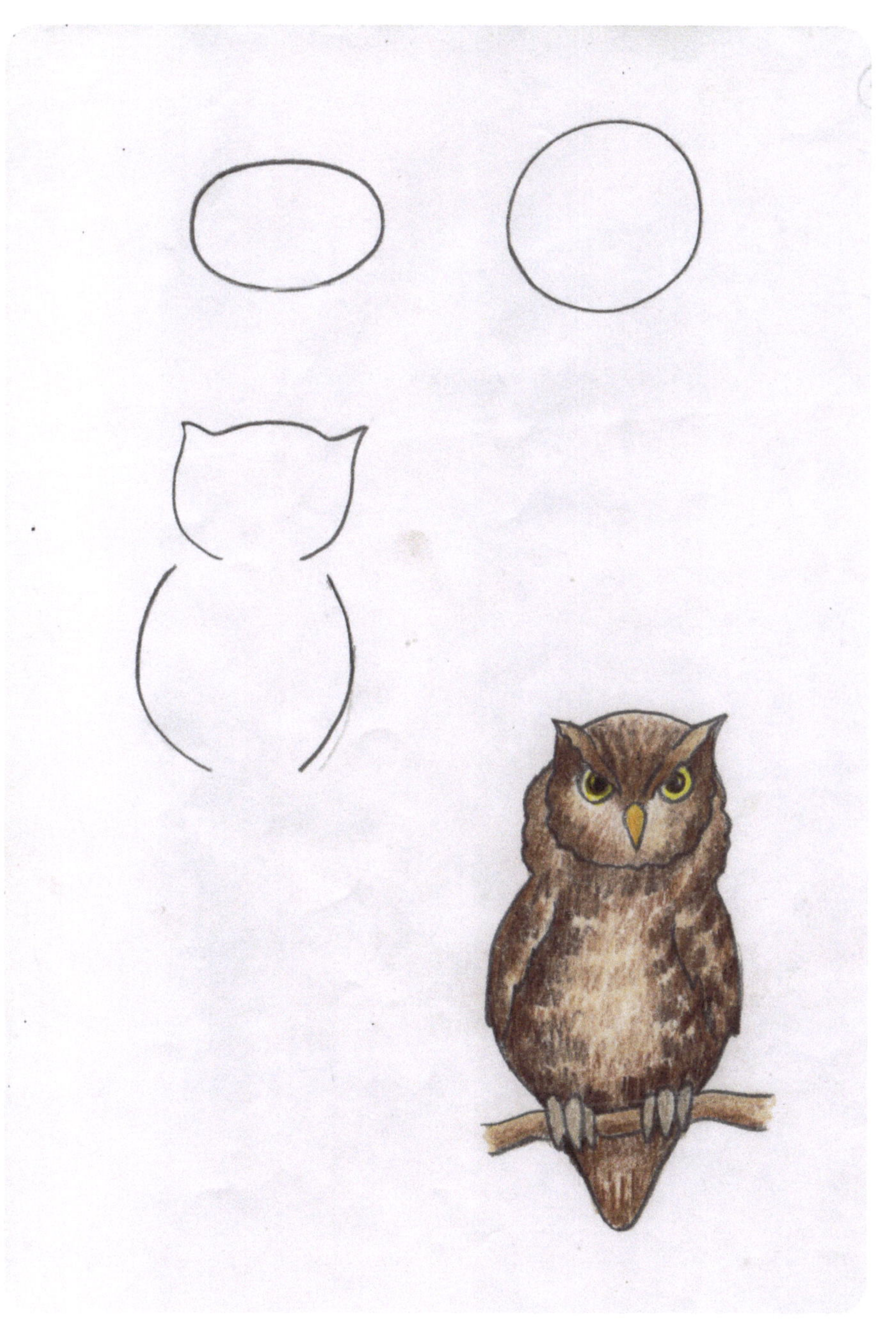

Here is showing how to draw Cockatoos in easy way. Take a look below steps.

Step 1: Draw a circle for head and draw a leaf shape for wing.

Step 2: Draw proper Cockatoo line and draw feathers, beak and eye too.

Step 3: Draw tail, wing, legs & tree branch etc.

Coloring: Here is using gray color and dark brown color. Fill with gray color in all area. Coloring should be in one direction. Shade with dark brown till half of gray color.

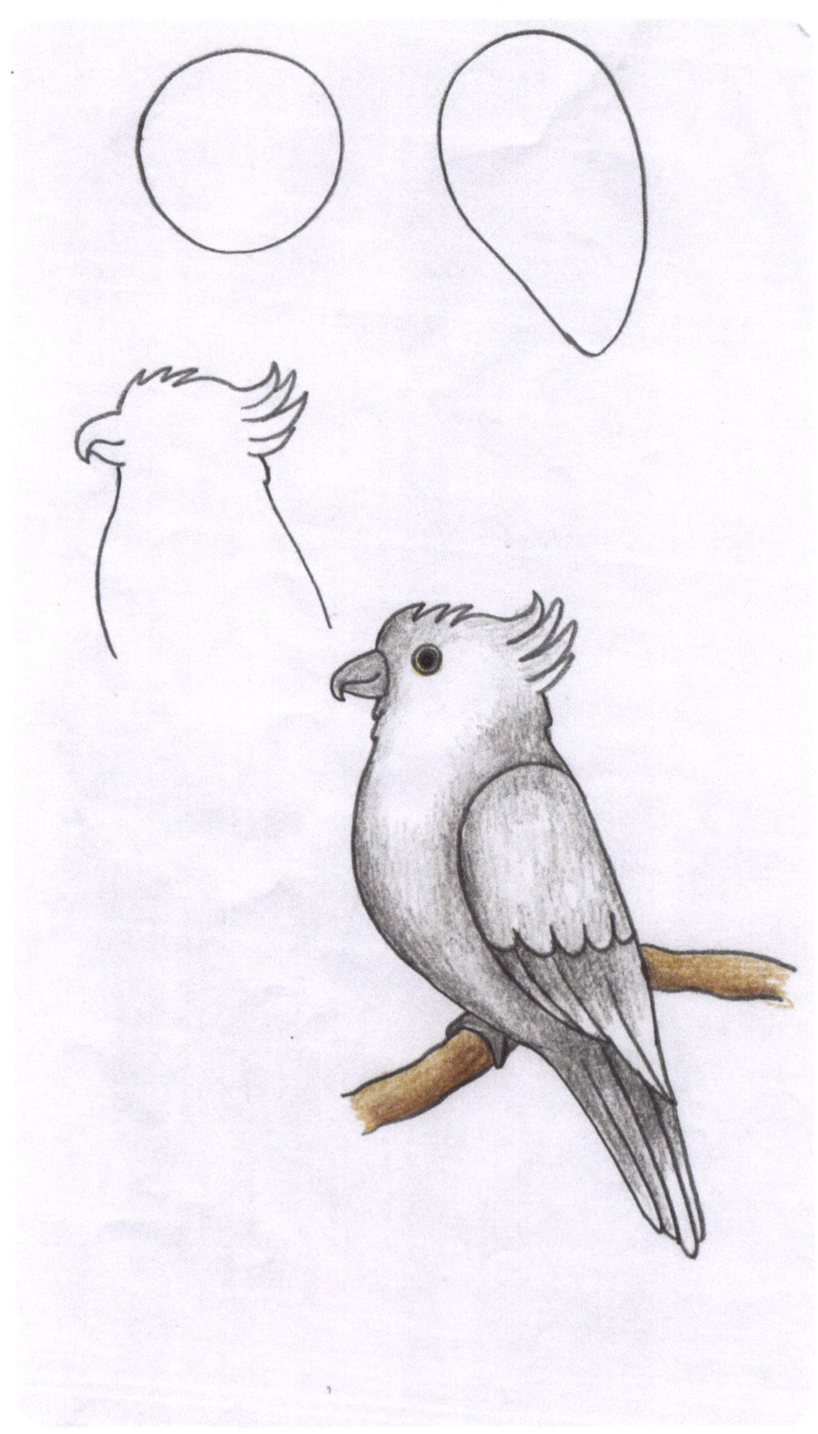

This is interesting picture, Toucan is colorful and different shape from other birds. Let see the steps below.

Step 1: Draw closure shape of bird beak, oval shape for head and leaf shape for wing.

Step 2: Join all the closure shapes but draw neatly to look like bird. Look at the given picture in the book.

Step 3: Complete drawing Toucan bird by adding eye, wings, design on the beak, legs, and tree branch etc.

Coloring: Here is using different color i.e. yellow, orange, gray, black and light brown. Fill yellow color in the beak in one direction then shade with orange color from the upper outline to downwards and down outline to upwards. Coloring should be merged well. Use yellow color for the eye and darken the eye ball with black color. Color orange near the eye and use gray color below the eye. Shade with gray color from the left side of white area (stomach). Color with gray in the legs. Color with black in all the rest of body and tail in one direction and should be same tone (medium tone). Shade with black color again over the black area, start shading from outer line till half of previous black color. Follow the given picture not to have doubt. Using light brown color in the tree branch. Try different position of Toucan if you are interested in this picture.

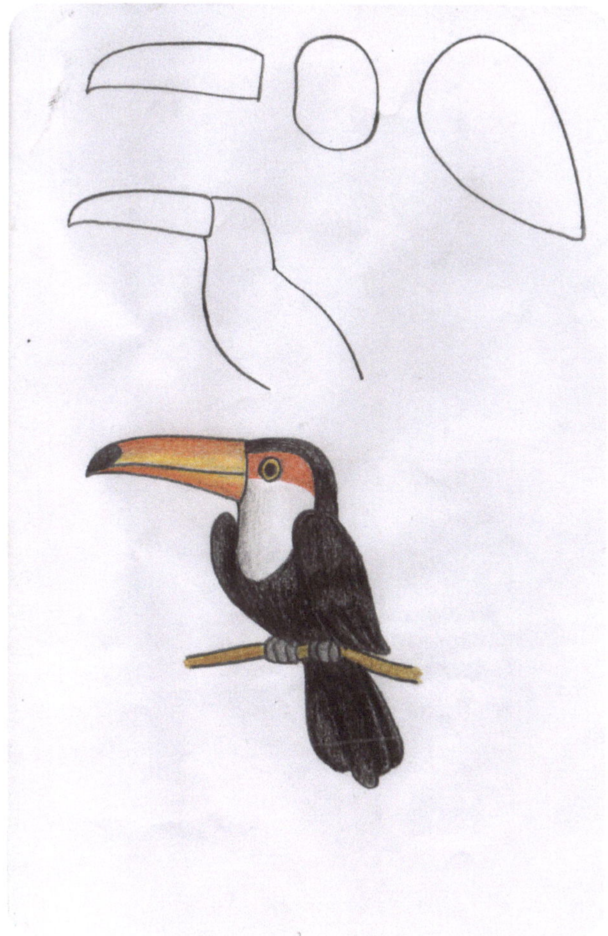

This is Igloo picture. Igloo is easy to draw but having closure shape will be easier. There are lot of curve line in Igloo. Let see the steps below.

Step 1: draw upside down U and a circle for the Igloo body.

Step 2: Join all the closure shapes and it should look real. Look at the given picture.

Step 3: Complete Igloo drawing by adding brick lines in the body of the Igloo and the entrance.

Coloring: Igloo is usually white because this house is in the snow area. So we can use gray and light blue color or any other color can be used. Here is using gray and blue color. Fill with gray color in all the areas in one direction and it should be same tone in all the area. Shade with gray color again over the gray area, shade from the outer line till middle part of the previous gray color. Continue shading with light blue color over the gray area till half of the 2nd gray area.

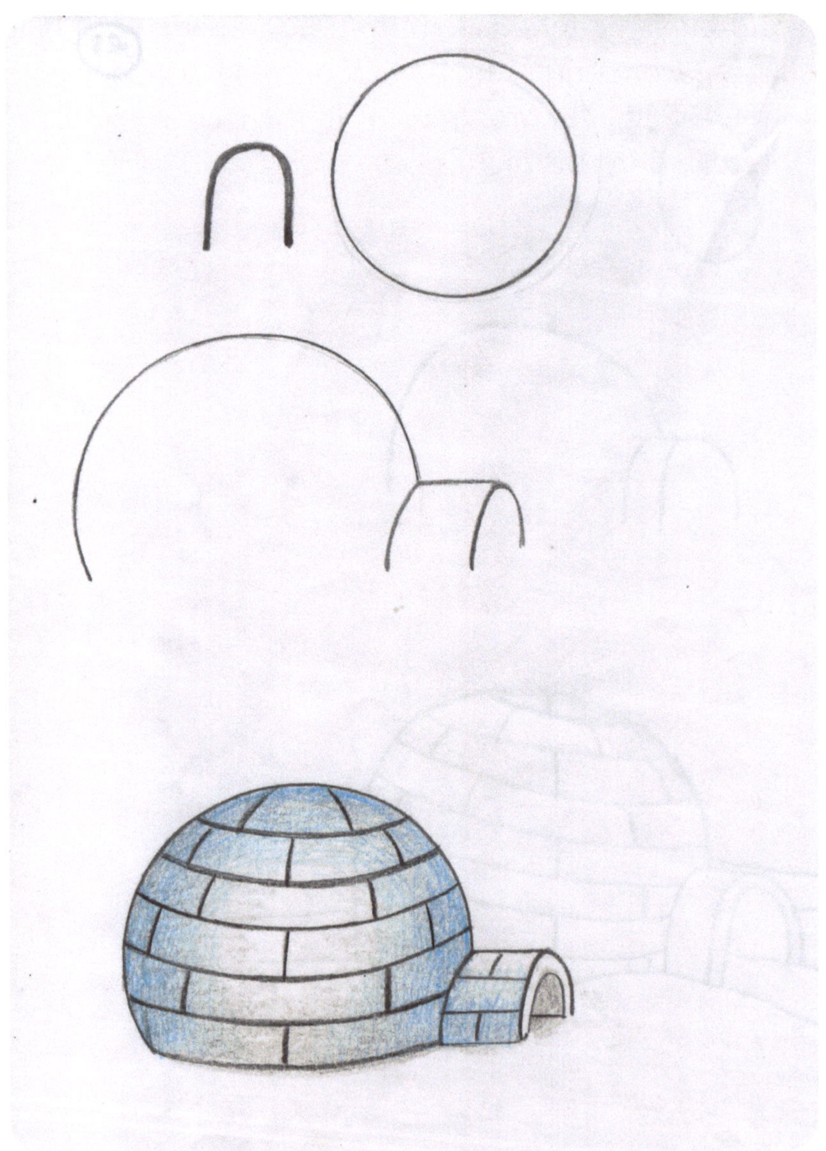

It is quite interesting picture and also easy to draw. Everyone can draw this picture. Let see the steps.

Step 1: Draw a circle for both head and body.

Step 2: Join the two circles, means draw like Snow man. Upper circle should be smaller than the lower circle because body should be bigger than head.

Step 3: Draw a muffler between the two circles and draw stick as a hand. Draw Hat over the small circle, Hat could be any design. Draw eyes and carrot for nose, also draw some button in the bigger circle. Look at the picture in the book. Try some other pose of Snowman.

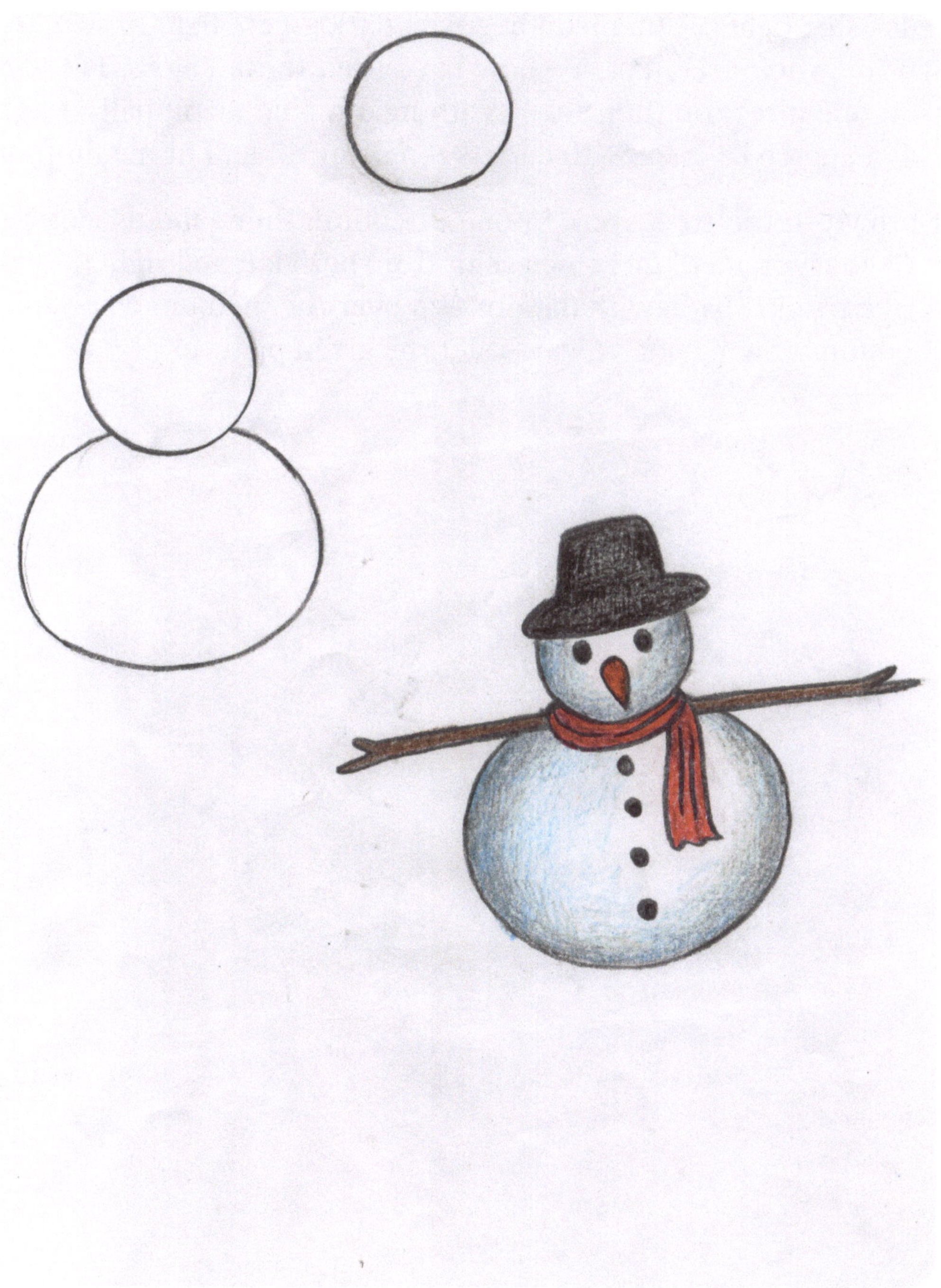

This page is showing quite different steps to show you different steps of drawing. Here is showing numbers and dots. There are dots with numbers i.e. 1,2,3,4,5,6,7,8,9,10,11,12,13, 14,16 and 17. Join the numbers, start from number 1 continue connecting the numbers till number 17. You can draw a tree after connecting the dots same as shown in the picture.

Erase the dots and numbers because you got tree shapes. Draw two curve lines for tree trunk. Look at the given picture to know the shape of tree. Draw big size of tree trunk at the bottom and small size at the top to look good.

Step 3: Draw V shapes at the top part of tree trunk to show tree branches and close the bottom of tree trunk to show ground.

Coloring: Here is using light green, medium green, dark green, light brown, medium brown and dark brown for whole tree. Let see how have used these colors. Fill with light green in all the areas in one direction then shade with medium color till half of light green area. Coloring should be merged. Shade with dark green color till half of medium color.

Fill with light brown in the tree trunk in one direction, there should not be paper white while coloring. Shade with medium brown color from both left and right outline towards the middle part of tree trunk. Shade with dark brown over the medium color and stop shading at the half of medium brown color. Always refer the given picture.

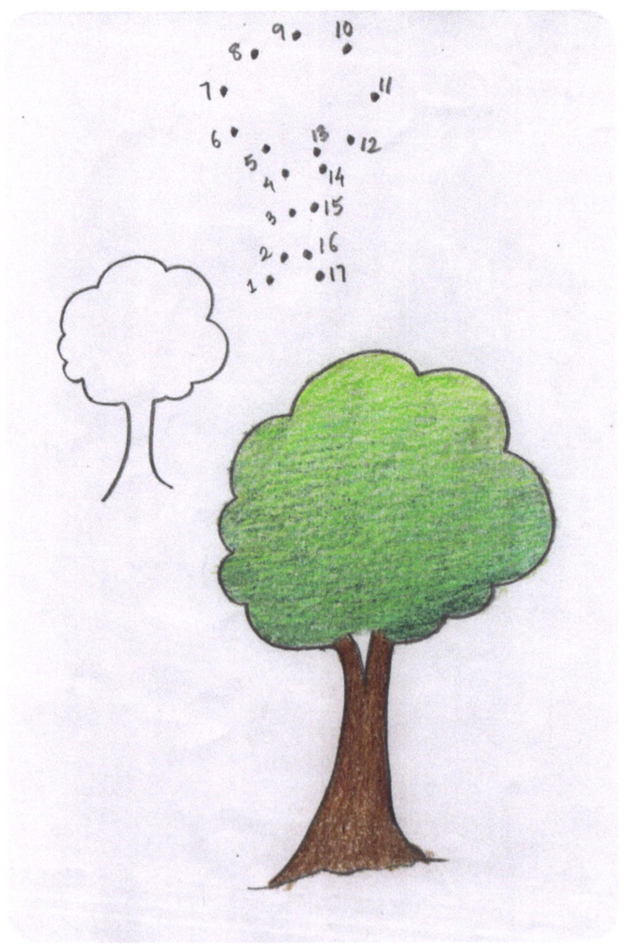

In this page is showing different steps of drawing. This step is totally different from previous steps. The picture in this page is clouds and the step is with short curve lines. Created different ways of steps in this book is just find out which is the best steps for you to use while drawing. Here is showing only two steps. Let see the steps.

Step 1: Draw short curve line in the shape of cloud.

Step 2: Join all the short curve lines to get cloud and draw another cloud just behind the previous cloud to look overlap the two clouds.

Coloring: Here is using gray color, light brown color and blackish brown color. Let see the steps of coloring below. Fill with gray color in one direction, make sure there should not be paper white. Sometimes can leave paper white if require because this is cloud. Shade with medium brown from the bottom outline till half of gray color and merge well. Shade with dark blackish brown over the medium color till half of the medium brown color. Similarly shade the behind cloud too but here is bit different i.e. shade more dark tone just behind the front cloud to show different layers. In the 2nd cloud is showing more dark at the left side because of overlapping clouds. Easily can figure out from the given picture.

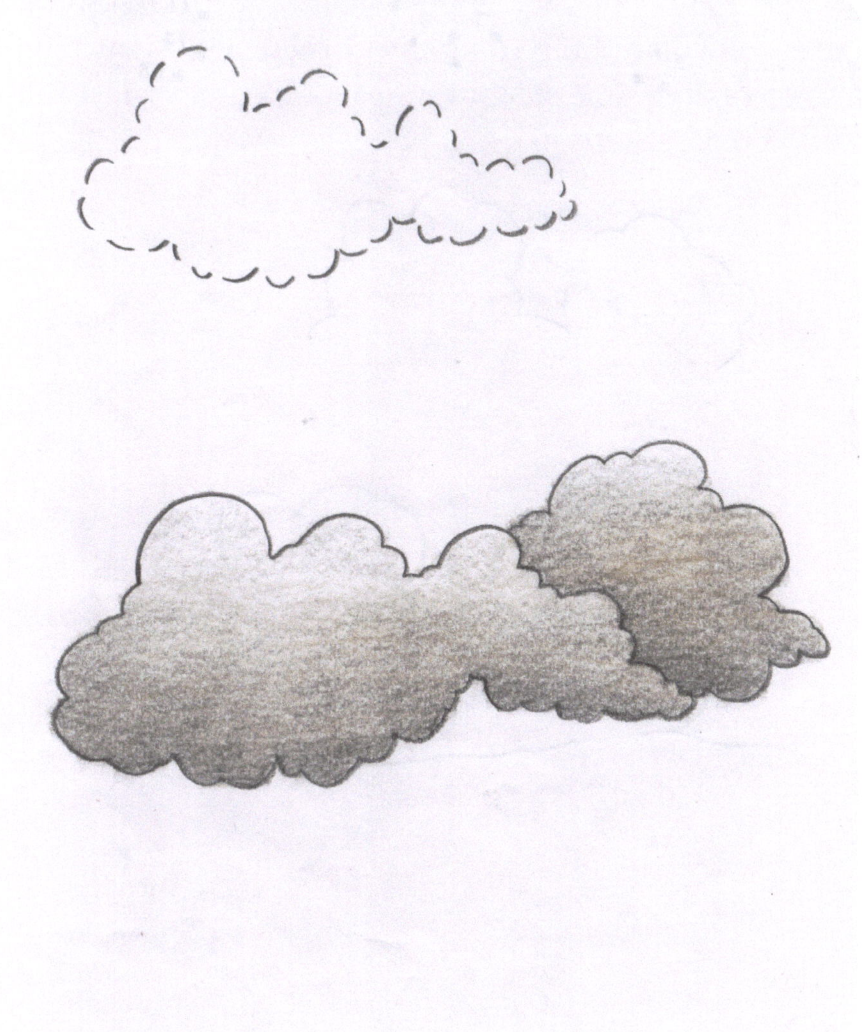

Here is showing steps with dots and numbers. Sometimes dots and numbers are good for children/beginners. It shows that quite easy while drawing. Let see how connecting the dots/numbers to draw Yacht.

Step 1: Follow the numbers and dots same as given in the book.

Step 2: Join the dots/numbers. Start from number 1 to 3 to 4 to 8 to 9 to 10 to 3 and the other side numbers to be connected is number 1 to 5 to 6 to 7 to 2 to 5 respectively. Then draw the body of Yacht.

Step 3: Draw a straight line (standing line) in between the Yacht cloth then draw bottom part of Yacht too.

Coloring: Try using different color for Yacht. Here is using light pink, medium pink, light brown, medium brown and dark brown colors. Fill with light pink color in one direction the cloth of Yacht the shade with medium pink color from both side of cloth and merge with medium pink color. Same should be done both cloths. Fill with light brown color in the bottom part of Yacht, keep in mind that coloring should be in one direction. Shade with medium brown color from the bottom part of light brown color and stop shading in the middle part of light brown color. Complete shading with dark brown color till half of medium brown color. Color light blue from left to right with light tone in the water then shade with medium blue color from the bottom part of water or just fill with only medium blue color for water. Always refer from given picture.

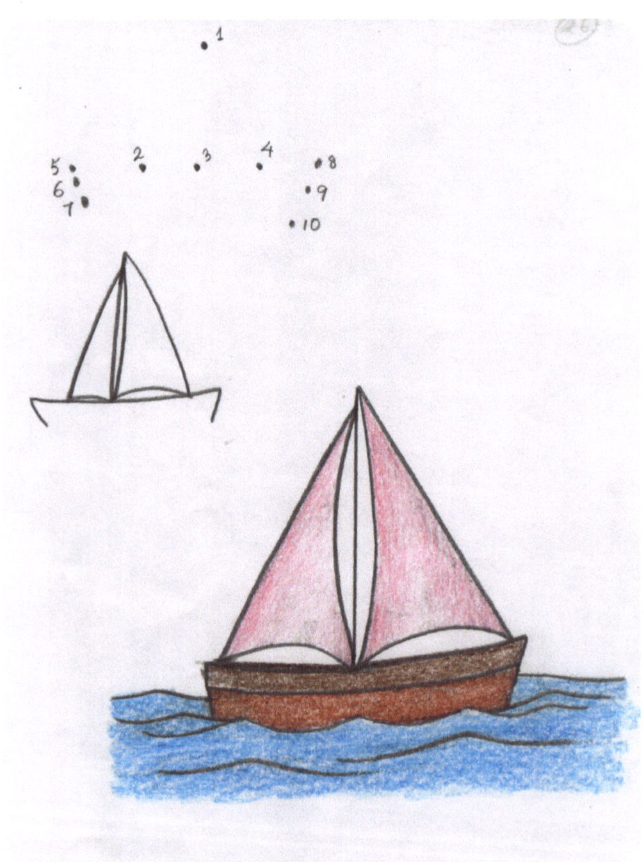

Here also showing dots and number. I guess some of you are quite interesting steps of dots and numbers, that's why showing here dots and numbers. Let see the steps below.

Step 1: Write numbers and dots same as shown in the picture.

Step 2: Connect the dots/numbers i.e. connect from 1 to 2 to 3 to 4 to 5 to 11 to 10 to 9 to 8 to 7 to 6 to 12 to 13 then 11 to 16 to 15 to 14.

Step 3: You can see a boat as shown in the step 2. Draw slightly curve lines at the bottom (from both sides of corner).

Step 4: Draw thickness of the Boat, inner depth line, inside seat etc. to complete the picture.

Coloring: Different colors can be used as your choice. There are many colors in Boat so coloring is up to you. Here is using light brown, medium brown and dark brown colors. Let see the steps of coloring. Fill with light brown color in one direction, however the Boat is horizontal so the best coloring direction is left to right direction. Then shade with medium brown color from the bottom till half of light brown color and merge well. Shade with dark brown over the medium brown till half of medium color. Fill with light blue color in the water, coloring direction should be from left to right because the water body direction is horizontal.

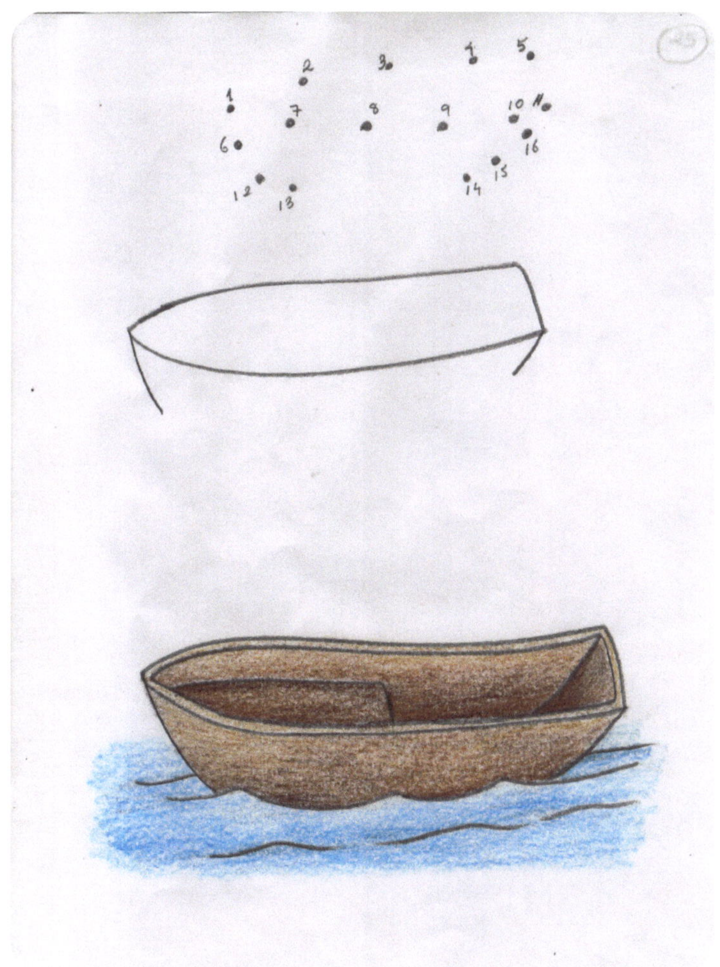

Here also showing dots and numbers for drawing Pine tree. Let see the steps below.

Step 1: Write numbers and dots as shown in this page.

Step 2: Connect the dots/numbers i.e. 1 to 2 to 3 to 1 and draw zigzag line from 2 to 3. Then connect 1 to 2 to 3 to 4 and 5 to 6 to 7 to 8 you can see a tree trunk after connecting the dots. Make sure the bottom part of the tree trunk is bigger than upper part of the tree trunk.

Step 3: Keep adding the tree leaves below the first steps of tree leaves till four parts, same as shown in the picture.

Coloring: Here is using light green, medium green, dark green, medium brown and dark brown. Fill with light green in all the leaves, the direction should be up to down because leaves direction is vertical. So follow the directions of object while coloring. Shade with medium green color from top to dawn. Start shading from just below the first part of leaves. Shade with dark green color over the medium green till half of medium color. Fill with medium brown in the tree trunk, here also direction should be top to dawn. Shade with dark brown over the medium brown color. Start shading from just below the tree leaves and stop at half of medium brown color. Try to draw different trees.

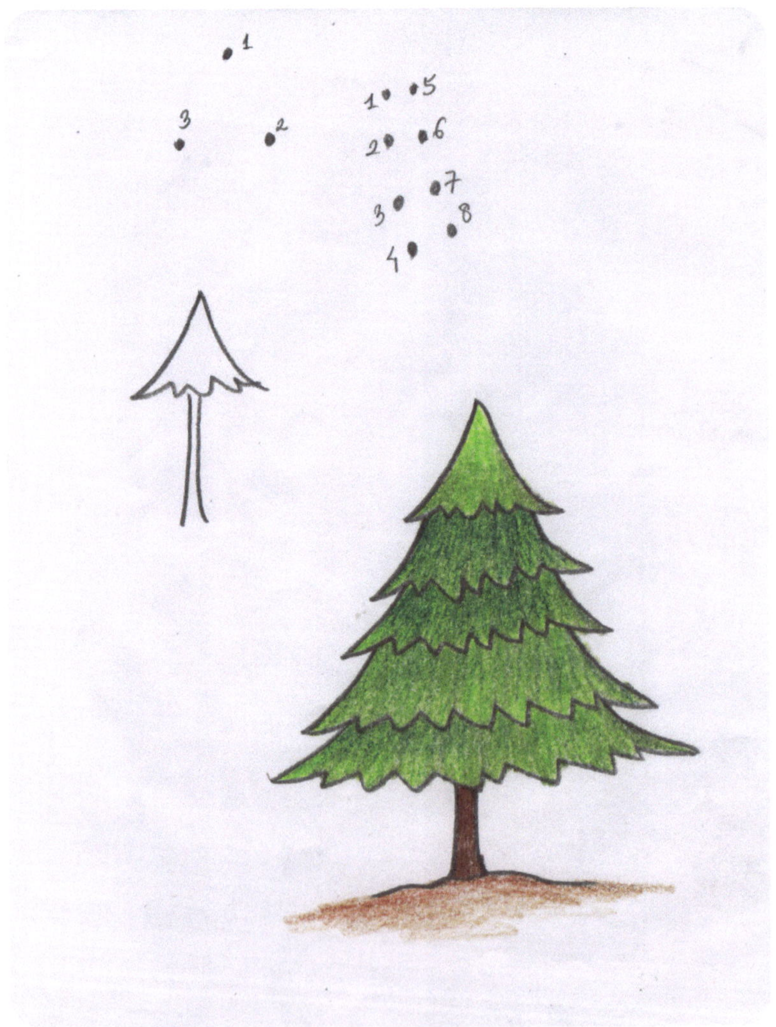

The steps of drawing Hut is showing here. There are different ways of drawing hut but this step is one of the best way of drawing Hut.

Step 1: Draw an oval shape and a box to start drawing Hut.

Step 2: Join both the shapes same as shown in the book.

Step 3: Complete Hut by adding windows, door and roof.

Coloring: Here is using light brown, medium brown and dark brown. Fill with light brown in one direction then shade with mssedium color from outline till half of light color. Darken the door and windows. Start coloring with medium color in the roof in one direction then shade with dark brown over the medium color. Finally shade with black over the dark brown.

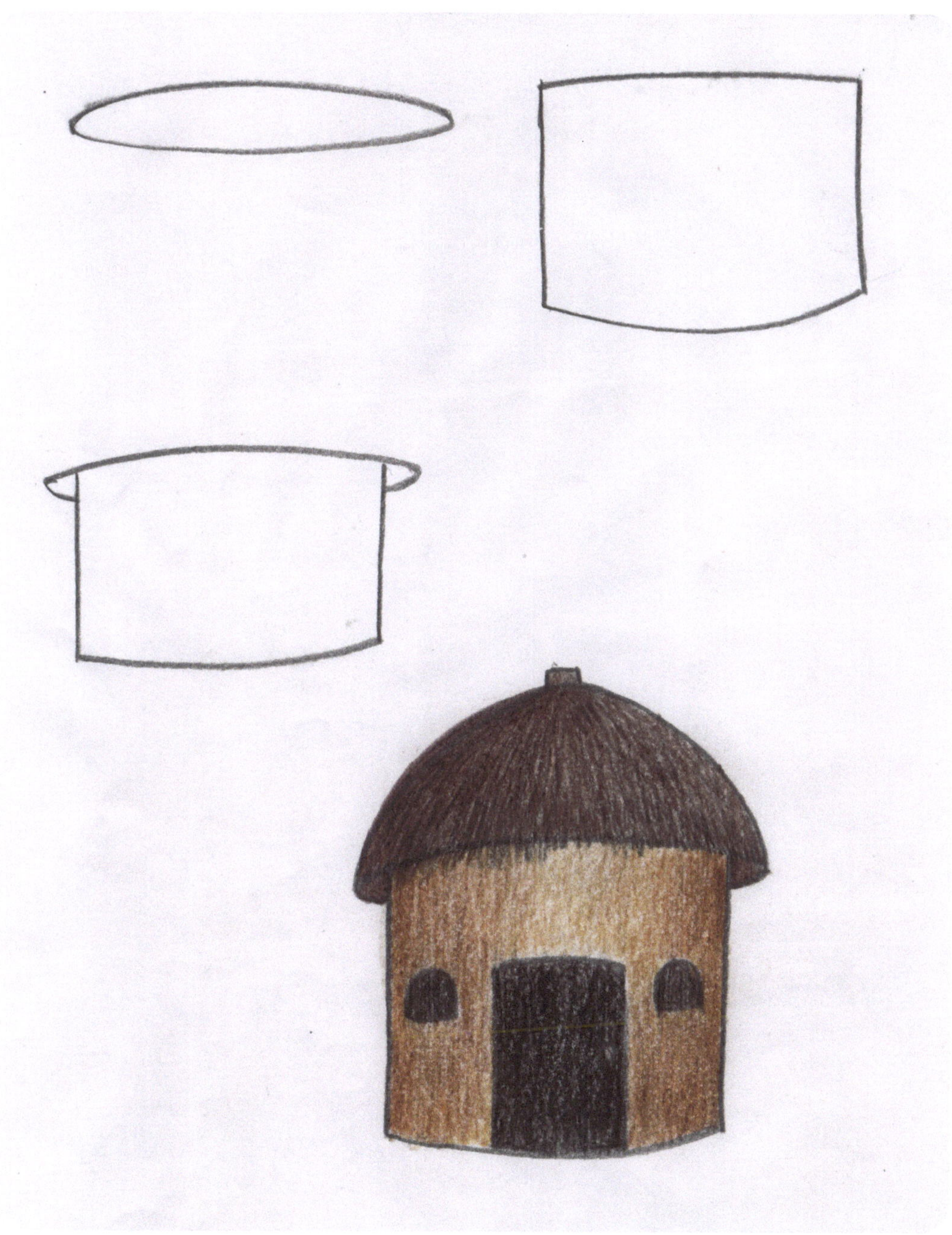

Here is showing how to draw wooden Bridge. Let see the steps below.

Step 1: Draw two curve lines same as shown in the picture.

Step 2: Draw another parallel line to the previous line and draw bottom part of bridge too.

Step 3: See the given picture and complete drawing.

Coloring: Any color can be used for Bridge. Here is using light brown color, medium brown color and dark brown color. Fill with light brown color in one direction then shade with medium color till half of light brown color, and shade with dark color till half of medium color. Make sure merge well all the colors.

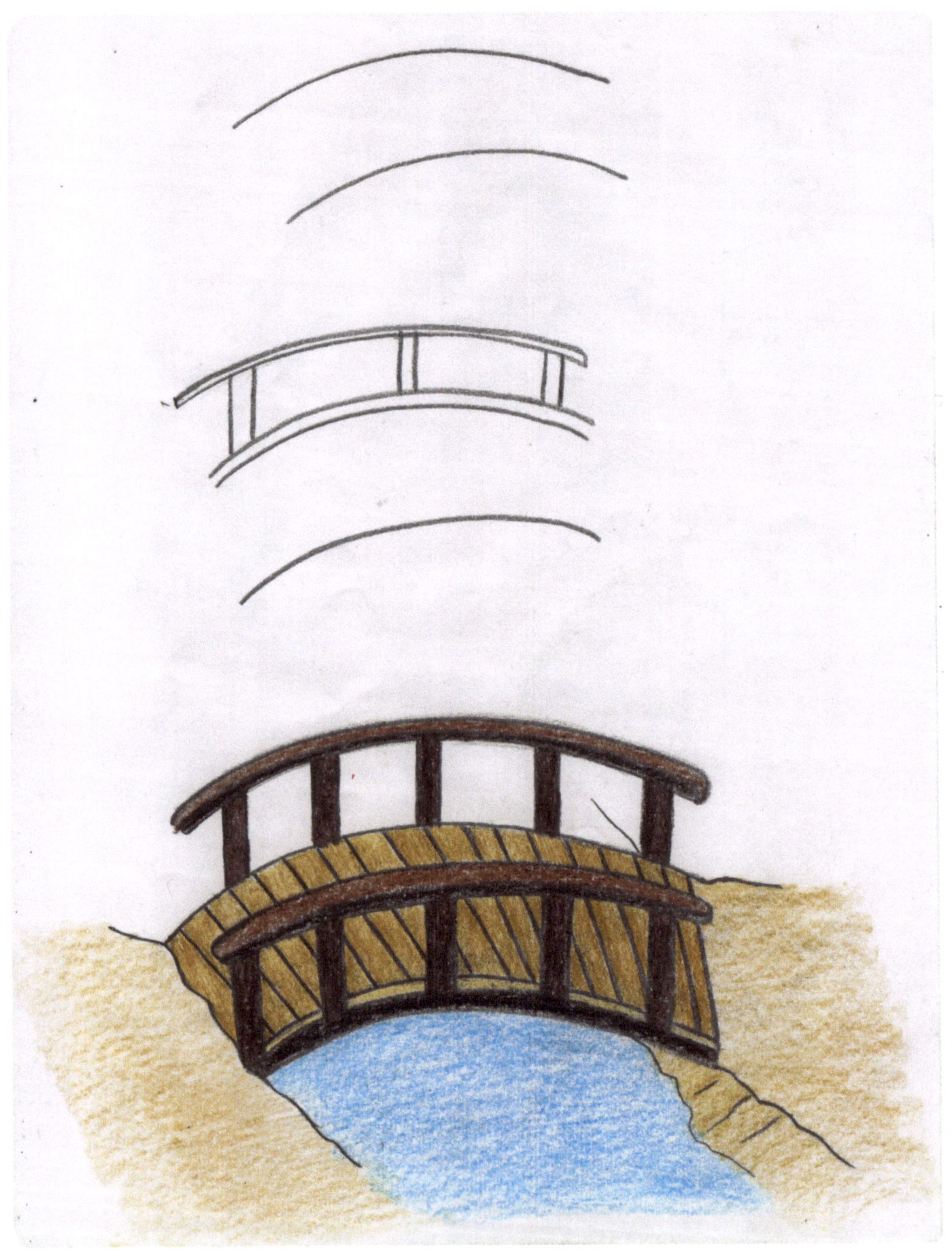

From this page I am showing you how can color landscape painting with color pencils. You are practicing from the page 1 to just before this page, so you can manage to do beautiful paintings.

Just sharing with you how should do this picture.

Sky: Start drawing from the front of hill then draw trees and behind hill. Fill with light yellow colors in the sky in one direction. Shade with dark yellow from right down to upwards in the sky, then do shading with orange color from the right side down to upwards till half of medium color.

1st Hill: Fill with light yellow color then use light green over the yellow color. Shade with olive green till half of light green then shade with medium brown till half of olive green. But look at the random shading (there are uneven shading) on the ground.

Trees: Fill with light yellow then do shading with light green from right to left direction because here light source is at the left side. Then do shading with medium green till half of light green and shade with dark green till half of medium green. 2nd Hill: Fill with light yellow then shade with light green till half of yellow color. Do upper part of the hill is light and down part of the hill is dark tone. Shade medium green till half of the light green color.

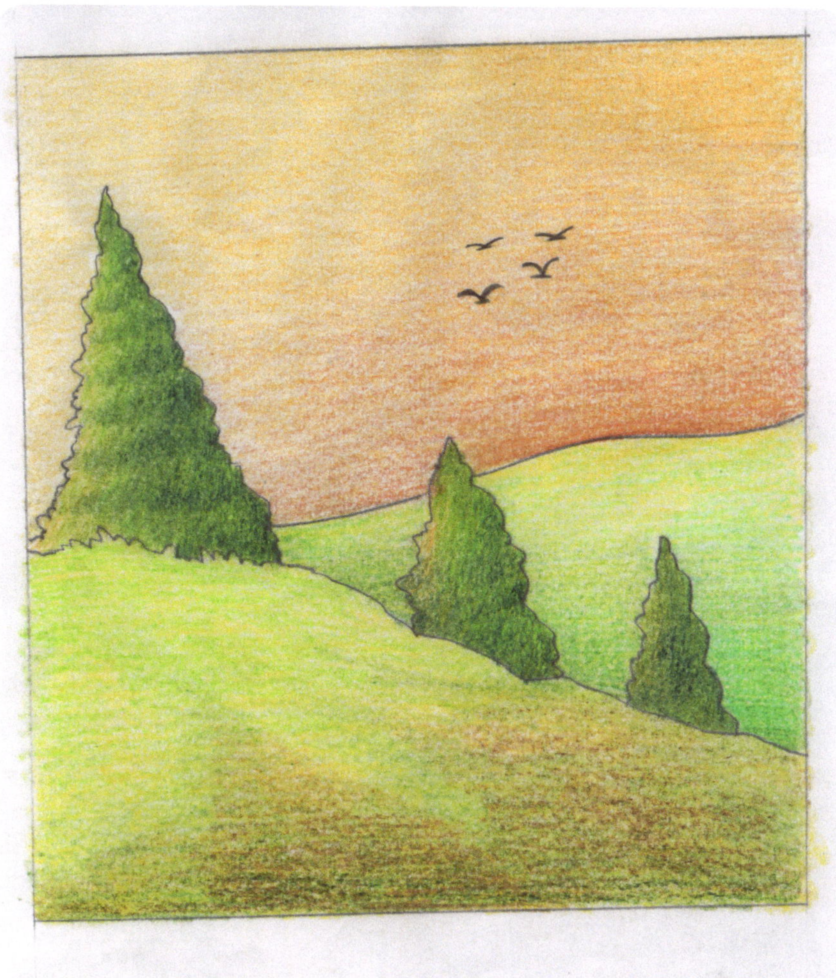

This is another landscape painting of color pencils. Draw House first then draw a line behind the House and trees then draw Hill at the back.

 Fill with light red color then fill with light brown color on the wall. Use black color on the door and window.

 Fill with yellow color in one direction then shade with light green till half of yellow color and do medium tone shading till half of light green. Then do shading with dark green till half of medium green.

 Fill with light brown in all area then shade with medium brown from the down till half of light brown color then shade with dark brown till half of medium color.

 Fill with light blue color in all the areas of sky except cloud area. Leave paper white for clouds, use medium blue color for shading till half of light blue area. I wish you can do best painting after seeing this landscape.

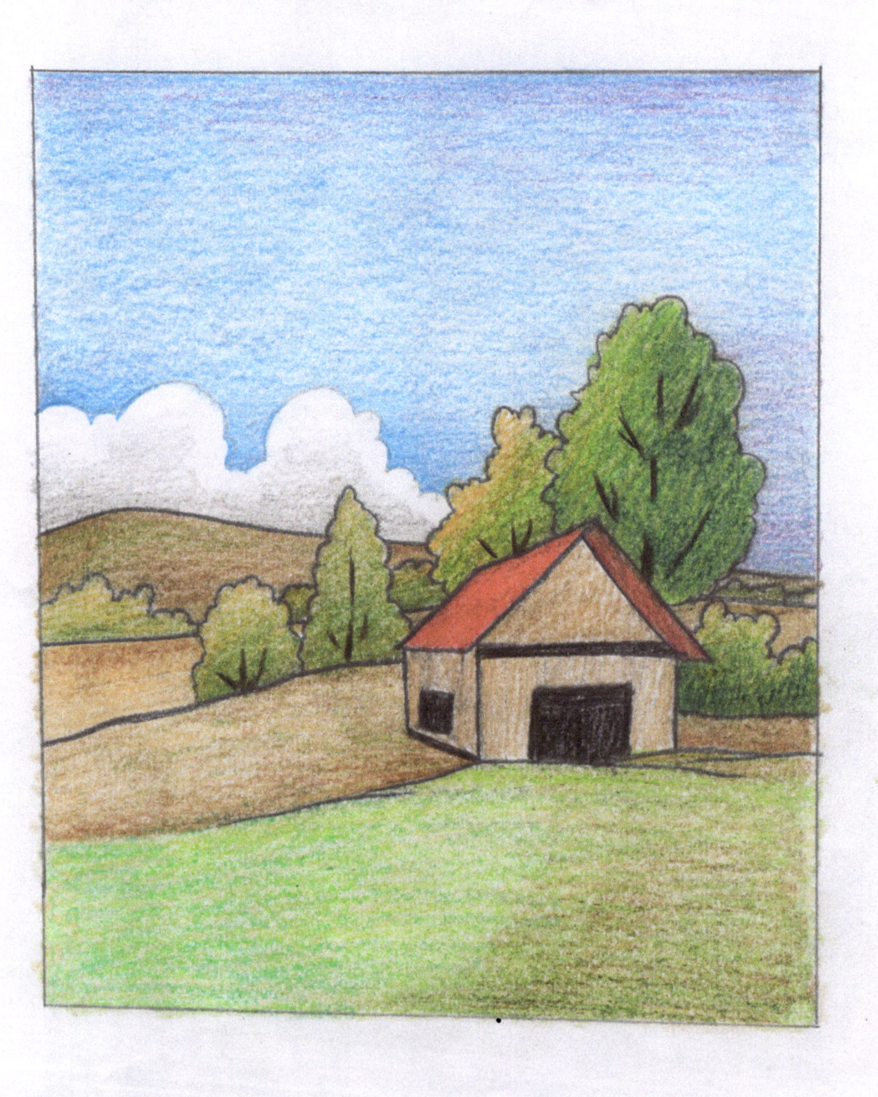

This painting is evening scene. Start drawing from the perspective fences then draw trees and bushes.

Coloring: Fill with yellow color in the sky in one direction then shade with medium brown from down to upwards till half of yellow color. Shade with medium brown then dark brown till half of each previous colors.

Fences: Fill with yellow color in one direction then do shading with medium brown color on the thickness of fences. Bushes and trees are same with previous pages so try same like previous pages.

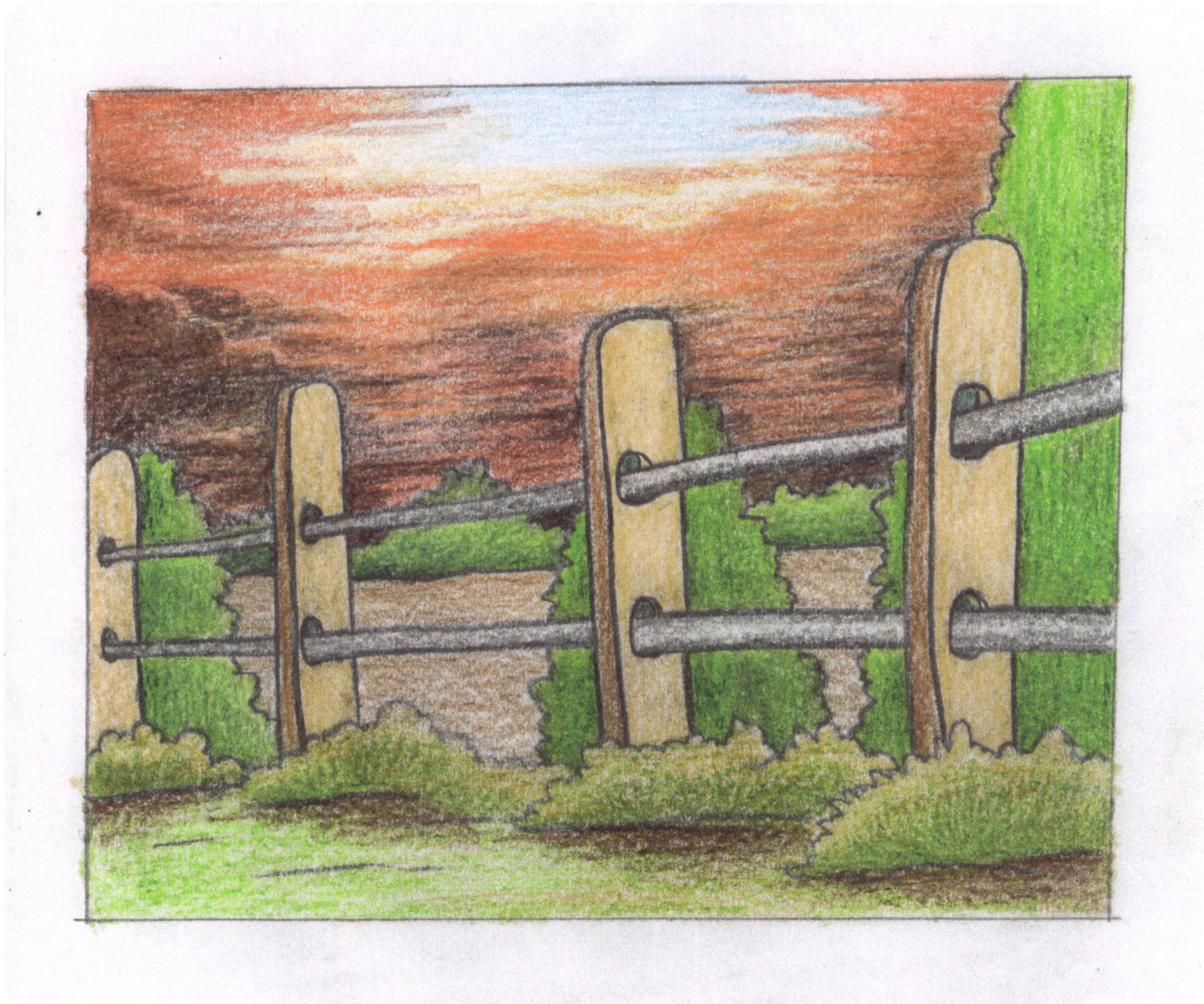

This quite interesting waterfall painting. Start drawing from waterfall then draw rocks in different shapes, trees and Hills.

Coloring: Fill with yellow color in the sky in one direction then do orange color shading from the down till half of yellow color and leave paper white for Sun.

Hill: Fill with medium brown from left to right direction then shade with dark green till half of medium brown color and merge well. Then do black color shading till half of dark green color.

Rocks: Fill with light brown color then shade medium brown color randomly as Rocks are in different shapes. So shading should be according to the Rocks shape. Shade with dark brown color till half of medium brown then shade with black color till half of dark brown color.

Waterfall: Fill with light blue but here have to color randomly according to the water flow, means some areas should leave light tone and some areas should do medium and dark tone to look like water flowing. Use medium blue color for water flow and shade according to the light blue color directions. These two colors are enough for Waterfall because Waterfall is light tone. There are rocks showing in between the Waterfall, it's just leave alternately while coloring Waterfall.

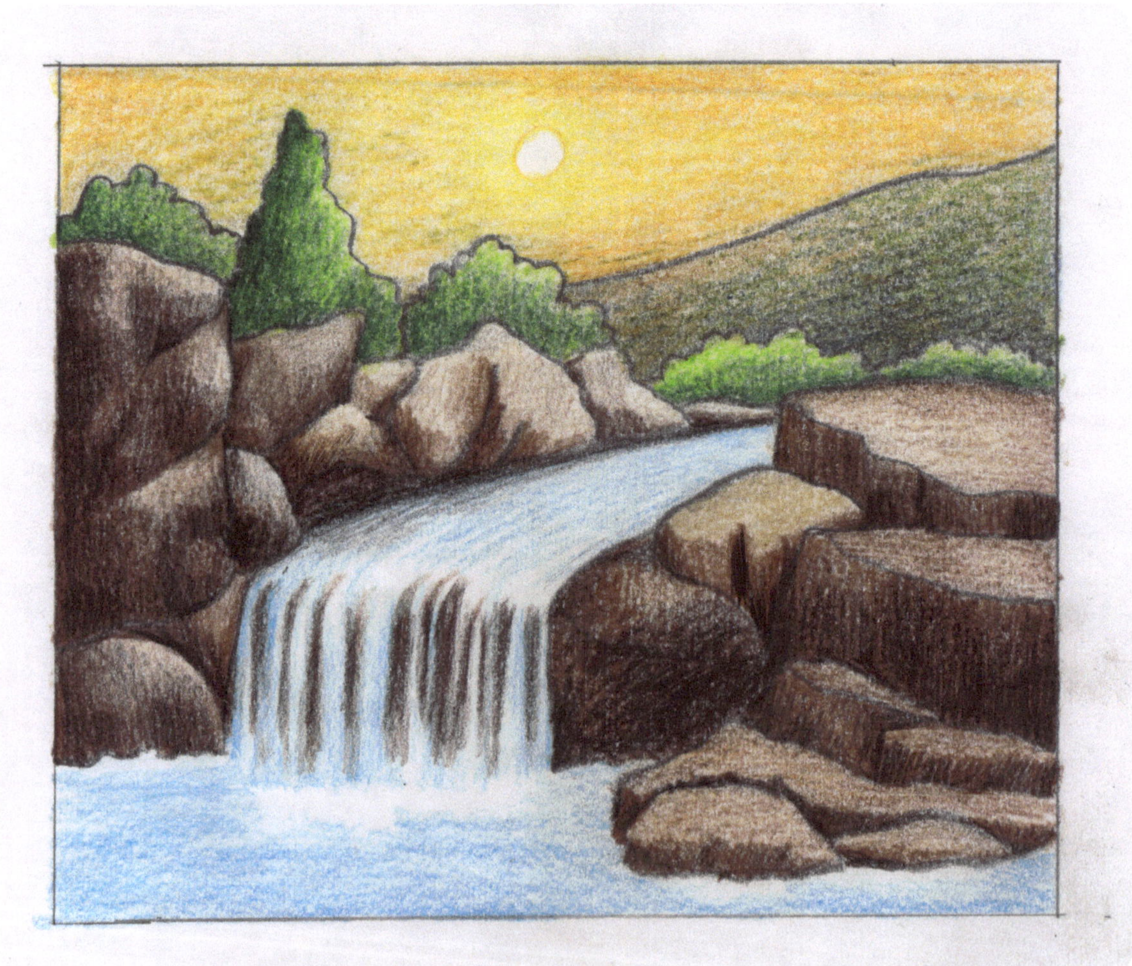

Here is showing reflection of Hills and trees in the water. Start drawing from Hills then trees and reflections in the water.

Coloring: Fill with light brown color in all the Hills, directions of coloring is according to the shape of Hills. Shade with medium brown till half of light brown then shade with dark brown till half of previous colors. Create some curve lines in the Hills to look real.

Reflection: Reflection should be something like upside-down objects. But coloring should be done with light tone because Hills and trees are at the far place. Reflection of trees should be done with medium and dark green color then do medium brown color for Hill reflections.

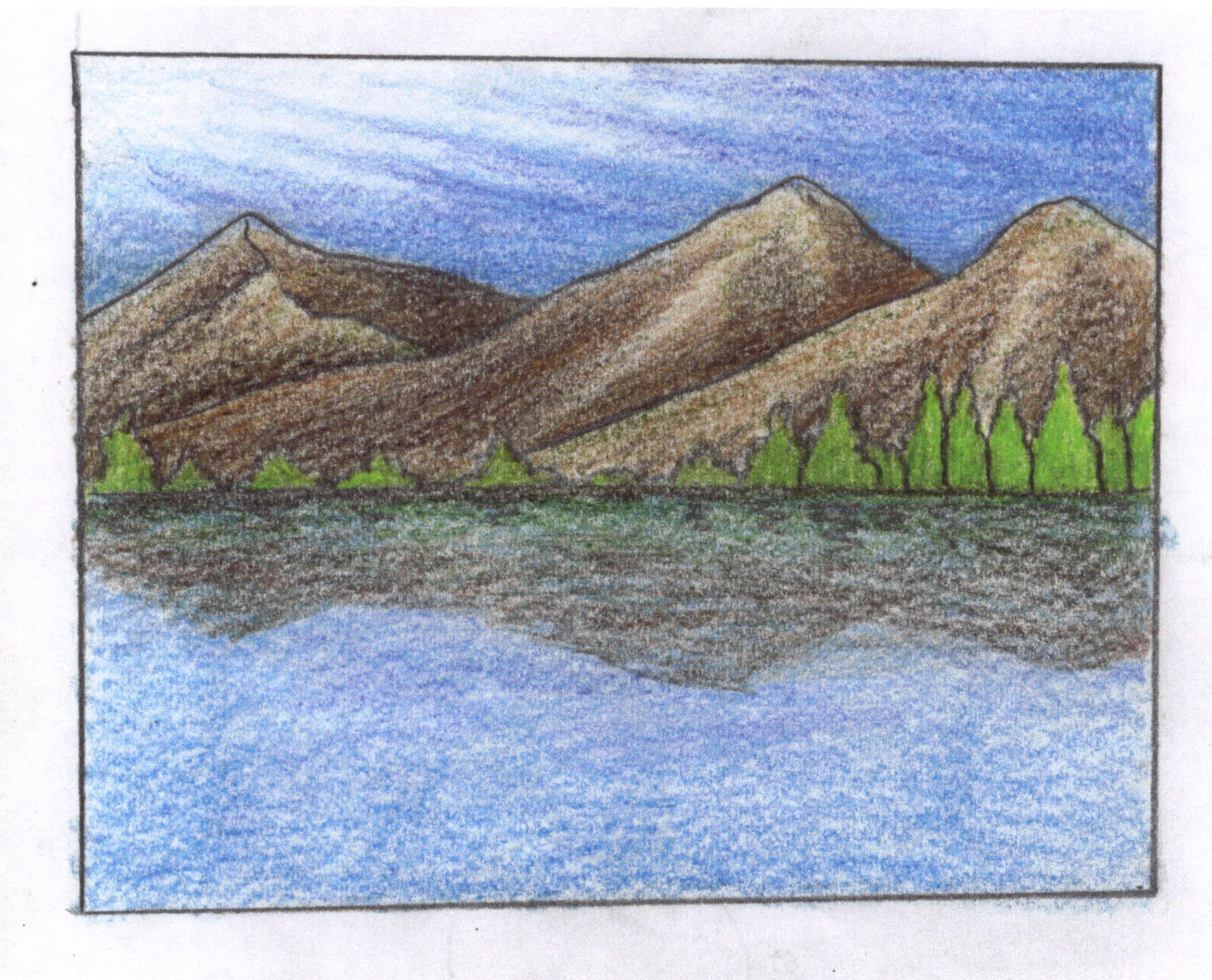

Some of outline drawings are here to practice. Try to add some background elements.

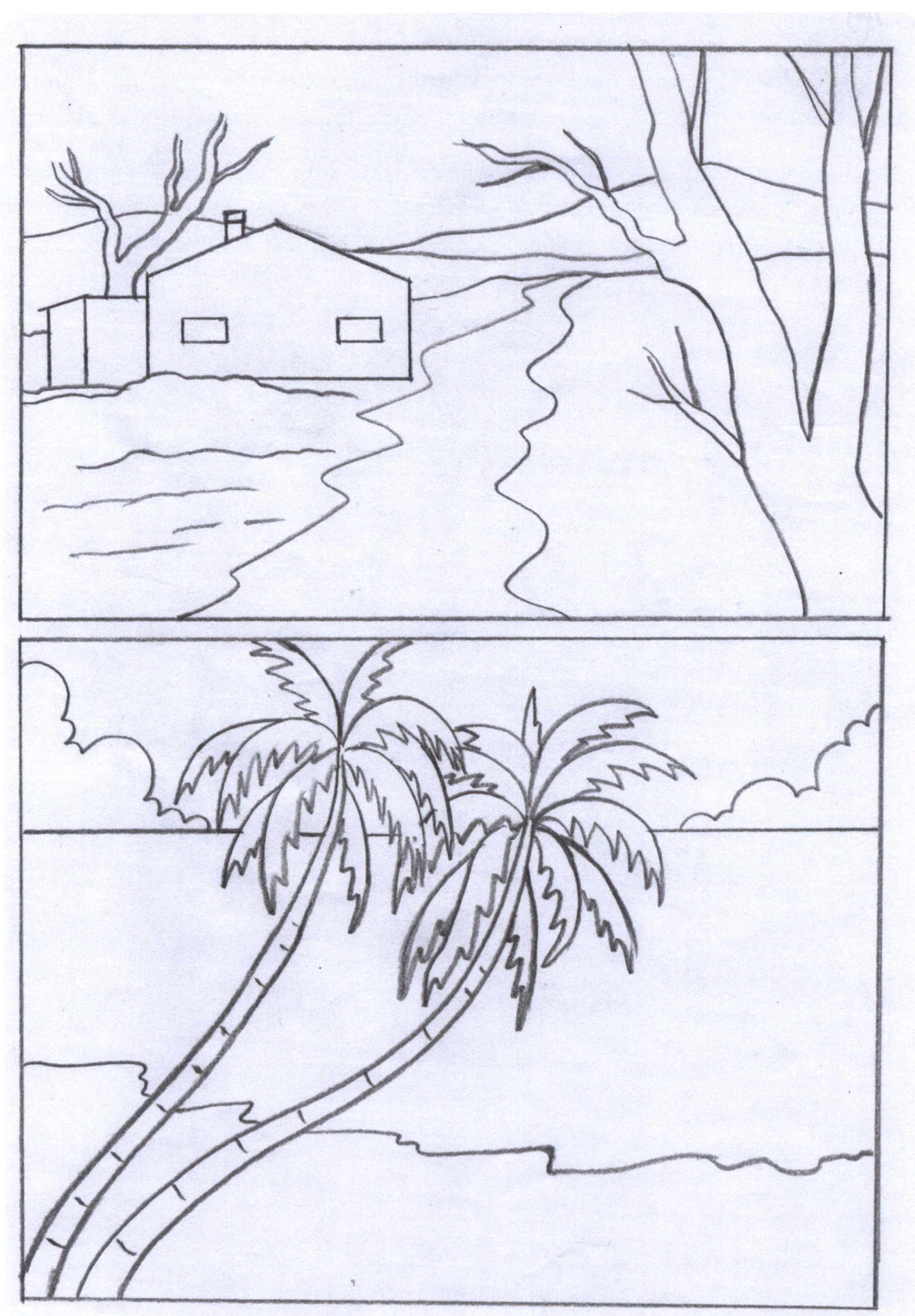

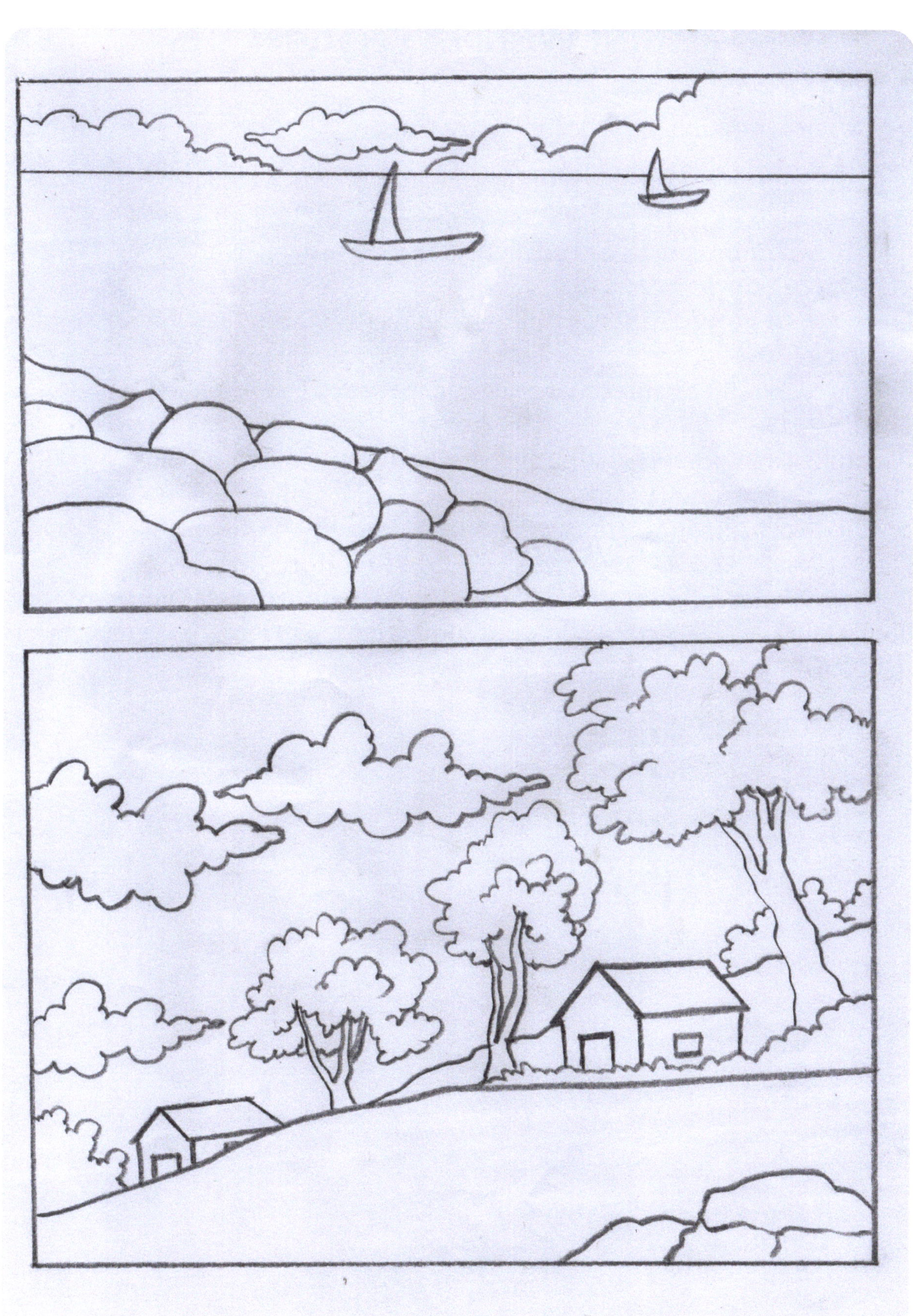

****Best Wishes Everyone****

My Awards & Recognition Received During My Career

1. 1st Position in International Painting Competition conducted by "Art Freaks People's Choice Art Contest" December 2007.
2. Special Award in International Painting Competition, conducted by "The Heart Of Art Contest" November 2016.
3. Silver Award in International Painting Competition, conducted by "Exhibition Art" November 2016.
4. Gold Award in International Painting Competition, conducted by "London Art Eye" January 2017
5. Top 100 Award in International Painting Competition, conducted by "Fine Art Universal" January 2017.
6. Best Artwork in International Painting Competition, conducted by "Online Art Contest" on 8th February 2017.
7. Young Talented Award from North East Zone Cultural Center Dimapur India 2007.
8. Gold Medal in All India Painting Competition conducted by "Vijay Information Hyderabad" March 2000.

About the Author

This is 3rd book, will give you a lot of benefits. In this book is showing you easy way drawing from the numbers/closure shapes and also easy steps of coloring is showing here. Trust me, it will definitely help everyone to learn become master in painting with regular practice.

Nongdamba Leitanthem was born in Imphal, Manipur (India) and the sixth child of Mr. Leitanthem Thoiba Meitei & Mrs. Leitanthem Prembala Devi. Due to his love in art, he started practicing Drawing and Painting since childhood. He has participated in many state, National and International – Level painting competitions and has won many awards and recognition. He has been doing lot of paintings with all medium.

This book is 3rd book published by him. He wants to share his knowledge and experiences in the field of art with all the people across the World who wants to learn drawing and painting through his books. This is his dream to publish books with easy steps of drawing and coloring where he can share and guide the people across the world.